Monica Dickens, the great-grand-daughter of Charles Dickens,
lives with her husband and two children in America, surrounded
by horses, cats and dogs.

Author of the famous *One Pair of Hands* and *One Pair of Feet*,
autobiographies of her early life, she has written such successful
novels as *Kate and Emma* and is also the author of *Follyfoot* and
*Dora at Follyfoot* (both published in Piccolo).

Her *World's End* novels are also available in Piccolo.

# Monica Dickens

# Talking of Horses

text illustrations by Margery Gill

**Piccolo** Pan Books in association with Heinemann

First published 1973 by William Heinemann Ltd
This edition published 1977 by Pan Books Ltd,
Cavaye Place, London SW10 9PG,
in association with William Heinemann Ltd
© Monica Dickens 1973
Illustrations © William Heinemann Ltd 1973
ISBN O 330 25114 7
Printed and bound in Great Britain by
Richard Clay (The Chaucer Press) Ltd, Bungay, Suffolk

To Hal and Mary,
who have shared this book with me,
as we have shared so many rides together

# Chapter 1

Come to the stable. Come to where the horses are, and the sweet, grainy, pungent smells.

A horse has the headiest, most satisfying scent of all animals. Mostly because of what he eats. But cows eat grass and hay and clover too, and there is less pleasure in their smell. A cow's breath smells of overfed babies. A horse's breath is a mixture of warm apples and chicken soup.

Everything to do with horses, their food, tack, bedding, smells very good. Everything feels good, the leather, a silky handful of oats, the cool metal of a bit, the smooth licked edge of the manger.

You don't need to have a horse or a pony of your own to know this fascination. There are three kinds of people in the world. Those who really dislike, and even fear horses. Those who can take them or leave them, and will only ride if they can leave the work to some maniac who actually enjoys it. And the maniacs who are infected with the disease of horses.

If you have it, it is for life. It is a disease for which there is no cure. You will go on riding even after they have to haul you on to a comfortable wise old cob, with feet like inverted buckets and a back like a fireside chair.

I knew a very old lady who still went out hunting. She rode side-saddle on an enormous horse called Trundle, who had a broad body with legs at the corners, cantering through the plough like a piece of furniture thrown overboard from a cruise liner on Gala Night, rolling away through the Atlantic swell.

The old lady's name was Lady Kesselring, but everybody – grooms, hunt members, village children, and men in berets following the hunt on bicycles with placards protesting that it was cruel – called her Lady Kessie. She wore a black habit with a top hat and veil, and she always had a big bunch of fresh violets in her button-hole. She potted them up from the garden in the autumn and kept them flowering indoors in her bay window with a compost rotted down from Trundle's stable.

Only Trundle. He would jump anything if he could take it slow and look at it. Lady Kessie hung on to the pommel with one hand and his mane with the other, and over they'd go. Each season, no one expected to see her out again, but she was always there at the opening meet, with the violets, and her skin like weathered tissue paper under the veil, and her tiny gloveskin boot in the stirrup below her skirt.

The doctor had threatened her with dire fates, like dying, which didn't seem to her so dire, since it was round the corner anyway. In

the end, Trundle went first, crumpling up one frosty morning half-way across a field full of rabbit holes and thistles. Lady Kessie sat by him until they came to take away his big square body, and then she got up and brushed off her skirt and pulled a spine of thistle out of her glove and announced she was going to give up riding and learn the piano. She was eighty-two.

When I can't ride any more, I shall still keep horses as long as I can hobble about with a bucket and a wheelbarrow. When I can't hobble, I shall roll my wheelchair out to the fence of the field where my horses graze, and watch them.

A man called Harry had a job at a riding stable. It was a small, neglected stable. The owner was more interested in his hotel, and so

Harry was left on his own to look after the horses and the stupid people in blue jeans and gym shoes, who thought you could hire a horse like you hire a bicycle, and learn to ride it as you went along.

The horses were thin and lifeless, not because Harry underfed them but because the owner bought poor quality hay and not enough oats. They were sluggish enough for the stupid people to ride, and there were no accidents. Except to Harry, which was brutally unfair. Riding out with a group of the stupid people, one of them straggled behind when they crossed a road, and Harry had to pull back to try and stop a car coming fast.

The car hit his horse, broke its leg and broke Harry's back. He was paralysed. When he came out of hospital, he was too weak to train for a job he could do from a wheelchair, so he went to a nursing home in the village where I live now, in America.

I looked out of the window one day and saw my four horses standing together by the far fence. That usually means there is a gang of small children holding out tufts of dusty roadside grass and going, 'Horsey, horsey,' which is annoying for horses, especially in hot weather when they want to be left alone; but they hang about in the vain hope there may be sugar somewhere.

I went out to tell the children to stay out of the field, because they climb through the fence and walk under the horses, or throw stones at them to see them run, and if they get kicked or stepped on, the parents say it is my fault.

It wasn't small children. It was a man in a wheelchair, in the shade of a tree, smoking a pipe and just looking at the horses. He sat there every day when it was fine. The horses made it their club place to stand and stamp and swish at flies and doze head to tail, while Harry watched them.

At the end of the summer, Harry's legs got worse, and they took him back to hospital and kept him there. His place under the tree is empty, and the strong, aromatic pipe smoke that kept flies away is gone from the air, and I am still chasing away small children who climb through the fence, or sit on the top rail and get their toes nipped. Once one of them slid on to Ben's back – cream-coloured Ben, who would bow if you tapped him below the knee – and rode him to the end of the field, where Ben put down his head and the child fell off. The mother said she would take me to Court for having a dangerous horse.

We ran an electric wire round the top rail to stop Guy cribbing on it and David leaning and breaking it, but the small children still climb through the middle and say, 'Horsey, horsey,' and hold out dusty grass.

Last night, I dreamed that all my horses came to me:
Chips, Jenny, Meg, Little David, Over, Tonia, Lollipop, Bow, Jacky, Puck, bay Peter, June, Titch, Robert, grey John, Bobby, Susie, Wendy, Ben who could bow, Ginny, Joe, Gingerbread, Ginger, Rosie, Specs, Guy, Trooper, black John, David Copperfield, Nancy, spotted Peter, Ben ex-racehorse, Oliver, Barney.
And other people's horses I have taken care of:
Jemma, Watermill, Dynamite, Ikey Mo, Robin, Nommie, Tortoiseshell, Genie, Honour Bright, Flag, Harvard, Showtime, Henry, Rudy, Peanuts, Tawny, Dianne, whose owner rode in the Olympics, and revolutionized our riding and broke all our jumps.
All the horses and ponies, the history of my life, jostling and trampling in the gateway of my dream.

Long ago, five million years before the Stone Age, a horse was eohippus, 'the drawn horse', about the size and shape of a whippet, with toes. It grew larger and swifter, always running from its enemies, because it had no weapons to fight with. The side toes became shorter, and the middle toe developed into a hard hoof, drumming over the dry Mongolian steppes a million years ago.

Primitive men hunted this horse for food. Then some roaming, plundering tribesmen realized that they were eating an animal who could help them to roam further and plunder more. Horses were pack animals at first. Five thousand years ago, they went to war, pulling chariots by awkward wooden yokes which pressed on the windpipe and jugular and made them throw up their heads. A horse can't pull fast with its head up, which is why it took four strong-necked stallions to pull one warrior in a two-wheeled chariot.

Then some inspired man saw the meaning of a horse's shape, and had the courage to jump on its back, and soon mounted swordsmen were riding rings round the unwieldy chariots. The Cavalry became supreme (it still takes precedence), the horse was admired and honoured, and the long, unending story of horse worship began.

To the Greeks, he was a god of beauty, half wild, half tame. Winged Pegasus, son of the goddess Medusa, carried the poets up to the firmament of fantasy. Poseidon the sea god sent forth the wonderful horse Arion, surging out of the foaming waves.

Now the great winds seaward blow;
Now the salt tides seaward flow;
Now the wild white horses play,
Champ and chafe and toss in the spray . . .

It was Hengist and Horsa who brought horses to Britain. That is why they are called horses. They brought horse worship too, and it stayed.

The spirit of that first man who had the vision to see why a horse was shaped like that, and the nerve to jump on its back and twist his fingers in its mane is still with us now, here where the horses are, sharing this strange, compelling partnership, working, or riding, or watching them over the gate of a field, chewing a blade of grass.

# Chapter 2

A horse turned out in a field is very different from a horse that is being led or ridden. Take him out on a cold day – there's hardly time to slip off the halter or unsnap the rope before he's off. He gallops, stops, spins round, stares, arches his neck to shake his head and gallops off again.

How beautifully supple and balanced he is! He can gallop from a standstill, stop dead, flick round a tight turn, slip, recover gracefully, swerve, change legs three times in three strides, this horse who has never managed a flying change with you. It is sobering to watch from the gate and realize how a rider limits him. Even a good rider. A meat-fisted sack of potatoes bouncing about throws him off balance completely, and the Sack complains, 'What's wrong with this stupid horse?'

Take the Sack to the field next time the horse is turned out, and let her watch how he handles himself without her.

He charges down from the top corner and stops with all four feet together, head high, snorting, tail up like a stallion. One eye is on the gate to make sure he is admired, and he snorts into the wind like a dragon, then trots out, sailing, this horse you can't persuade into more than an apology for an extended trot. With the Sack on board, he positively shuffles.

Incidentally, the Sack has no business riding your horse, if she won't ride properly. Perhaps it is not your horse, but one you both ride. Perhaps it is the Sack's horse, in which case her parents have more money than sense, and should have had her taught to ride before they inflicted her on a horse.

Watch a horse's natural movements. It helps your balance and your hands to remember how freely he moves without you.

In my house where I live now, there are paddocks all round, and so you can see horses out of nearly every window. From the bedroom window on a summer night, I can see them wandering in and out of the patches of flat white light and the deep shadows of the moon. I can hear them rustling and blowing, on damp nights coughing the strangled one-syllable cough – that's John, bred far inland, who has slight chronic bronchitis from living near the sea. Sometimes they suddenly start racing in the middle of the night, a thudding stampede for no reason, unless it is ghosts.

In the daytime, they come to graze near the fence which is only twenty yards from the window over my desk. Charles Dickens had a kitten called Williamina's Son, who used to paw at the candle flame to try to put it out, so that Dickens would stop reading and take some notice of him. Guy used to get my attention by cribbing and windsucking on the fence rail to annoy me.

Long yellow teeth, worn crooked from years of grabbing on to edges, fastened on the top rail, front legs braced, neck arched, eyes and ears thoughtful, Guy would suck in a gob of air with a disgusting grunt, lick the rail gratefully and start it all again.

Why no cribbing collar? Short of having it tight enough to choke him to death, he was too far gone in his habit for it to be any use. The neck muscle behind the ears becomes tremendously strong from constantly tensing as the jaws grab. Guy, who was a puller anyway, became harder and harder to hold. They say that the only hope for incurable cribbing is to cut that neck muscle, which seems a bit drastic.

David, who is a great fiddler, and can open bolts and latches, attracts my attention by flipping the iron loop of the gatepost up and

down. The gate is chained shut, to foil him, so he puts a large hoof on the bottom bar and rattles it back and forth.

John relies on dropping his head and staring at me between the fence rails. Once when I was in the kitchen with my back to the glass-panelled door, I had that feeling in my spine of someone calling me silently from behind. I turned, expecting to see a neighbour crossing the lawn, and saw John, who is a Western horse and therefore familiar with the unspoken messages of the wild, standing by the empty trough and concentrating on me to come out and fill it.

Most horses are quite unenterprising about getting out of fields. They have brainwashed themselves to stay within a fence and hedge, even though they could easily jump it if they gave their mind to it.

Cleverer horses spend a great deal of time, especially in winter when the grass is less interesting, working on escape routes. They break fences, open gates, push through weak spots in the hedge. Ginny, the New Forest pony mare, had a colt called Joe who used to squeeze through the fence, so she had to break a rail to go after him. When we ran a strand of electricity (safer than barbed wire) between rails, Joe bit through it and was activated by the mild shock to charge out and eat a bed of young lettuce.

When horses do get out (the telephone call always comes about two a.m. when you are deeply asleep, 'Your horses are out again!'), they may not wander far, but if they go over people's gardens, you'll hear about it, and if they get hit by a car, you'll know tragedy.

An American called Frank had some fancy Saddlebred show horses. The groom forgot to bolt a door, and Pasadena's Pride lifted the latch and disappeared. She was gone for two days . . . three days . . . four days. They had the Boy Scouts out, the Guides, the local Pony Club, policemen, firemen, even a helicopter to scout over the wooded land. Frank was just going to claim the insurance, when the girl groom, who had been sacked, went out to an unused shed to get her suitcases, and saw Pasadena's Pride fifty yards from her stable, her expensive initialled rug caught fast in the thicket.

The horse was famished and a bit scarred up. She had rubbed her neck and tail, but her mane and the top of her tail were hogged anyway, in the ugly way these poor neurotic three-gaited Saddlebreds are shown. Their feet are grown very long and heavy, to make them step high, lifting the weight. A jingling chain or a bracelet of rattling beads is hung round the fetlock, so that they pick up the foot even higher, trying to get away from the rattle. The depressor muscles at the top of the tail are cut and set high in a brace which the horse must wear nearly all the time. If the tail is a bad colour, it gets dyed. If it's skimpy, it wears a wig.

Frank's horses never went out of the stable, except for schooling and shows, and they were a mass of nerves. The girl groom, who got her job back, rode Pasadena's Pride over to my house one day, and we turned her out while we had lunch, and the poor thing nearly went mad with joy. The girl couldn't catch her for three hours, and thought she would lose the job again.

No horse should be kept always in a stable, and never turned out. People fancy that they can keep a pony in the garden shed, or staked out on the tiny back lawn, but it won't work that way. There must

be some enclosure to turn the pony out, or at least a large space and a long rope so that he can move freely round the stake.

'I'll exercise him every day,' says the child who is given one of these toolshed ponies. But pretty soon it's either too hot or too cold or too wet, or there's too much homework or too much to see on television.

'A pony all my very own!' Doting parents buy it like a bicycle. It may be a raffle prize at a charity bazaar, a competition prize from a newspaper. In America, you can order it from a catalogue, like a frying pan or a pair of trousers. At first, the child half kills it with love and stroking and sugar, and riding it double with a friend, dressed up as cowhands. Then it gets boring, because it is probably a second-rate pony anyway, palmed off on parents who know nothing except that little Melissa wants a pony all her very own.

'She must take care of it all by herself,' declares the father, priding himself on right upbringing; but really it's all wrong, because no young child can be left unsupervised to look after a pony.

It moulders in the shed or on the short tether on the bare lawn, with a tight halter rubbing lumps of fur off its face. Little Melissa gives it a small pail of water twice a day because she doesn't know it needs at least five gallons, and a haphazard quantity of oats because no one told her about hay.

Soon it is unridable, so she doesn't ride it. One day it kicks dear old Dad, and he sends it to a sale, and little Melissa can cry all she wants, and the pony can only hope for better luck.

Even if a horse were exercised every day, which is impossible all the year round, it is not the same as running free. A hard-working hunter spends most of the summer wandering the lush grass. Show horses are allowed to slack off in a field between seasons. When pit ponies worked in the coal mines, they regularly came to the surface for two weeks out at grass.

Given his choice, a horse would rather be out than in. If you had a range of loose boxes opening on to an enclosed field, and you left the doors open, you would invariably find every horse out in the field, even with food still in the manger.

There would probably be one horse who knew which of the others was leaving food, and would nip in to clean up. The owner of that box would then go back to it in a sour grapes way, and there would

be a lot of kicking and banging and squealing and one of them would come flying out with a large piece of hide torn off him.

Jacky and some others were kept out all winter in the field by the church when their children were away at school. They had an open shed where they could shelter and eat hay. After a night when it had snowed heavily, I found Jacky lying contentedly out in the middle of the field, mounded with snow like a blancmange, his eyelashes frosted, his whiskers iced. He looked like an animal a chef will mould out of ice to decorate a buffet table at a grand affair. Under the snow, he was generating the tremendous body heat that a healthy horse can cook up. You could warm your hands in the steaming cloud of his breath.

In Siberia, they hose the horses down with water, so that it will freeze, and insulate them against the cold.

Unless they are being hunted, or shown, or there is something for which they need to be kept fit and spotless, horses and especially ponies are better out as much of the time as possible. Even if they are clipped, or are wearing rugs to keep the winter coat from growing, they can go out in the cold in a New Zealand rug, which is weather-proof and will survive rolling.

Rolling is one of the most important things in a horse's life. He craves it like a passion. He needs it desperately. So desperately some-times that a pony may try to go down to roll with you on top. Keep his head up and kick if he starts sagging. If it's too late, take your feet out of the stirrups as he collapses under you, and step off before he rolls on your leg.

Barney was picked in the first six out of a big class of Working Hunter Ponies. After they had jumped, they were lined up without saddles for the final placing. While the judge was inspecting the pony ahead of him, Barney lay down and had a good roll. He got sixth.

Rolling, to a horse, is a super grooming, although to the person who grooms him it is the opposite, since it undoes a lot of the clean-ing work. But to a horse, rolling is self-grooming, an instinctive need, like a monkey's need to be cleaned by another monkey of fleas and flakes of dead skin.

When you bring him in from a ride with sweat on him (almost dry sweat, of course, since you will have walked him dry on the way home), it's just as effective to let him out to roll and potter about until he's cooled off before his feed, as to spend all that time rubbing him down and walking him about. More effective, from his point of view, he gets the smell of you off him.

He doesn't only roll to get rid of the itches and sweat, but to get rid of the smell of person. However much he loves you, and likes to lick the palm of your hand and mumble his lips over your hair, he must purify himself of human contact, as a cat will wash itself after you have picked it up.

From your point of view, the main difference between grooming a horse and letting him groom himself by rolling is that one gets him clean and the other gets him dirty. Apparently the horse, like the sparrow and the hippopotamus, whose name means 'water horse', has a basic need for dust and mud.

Watch him pick a spot to roll. He puts his head down, paws, turns round like a dog making a bed, bends at the knees and hocks, changes his mind, moves to another patch which smells of someone else's rolling, sniffs, paws, moves on again to a muddier place, sags, collapses with a grunt and a thud that echoes through the ground on

a cold dry day. Over he goes, balancing on his spine, displaying the seam where his coats meet down his wide stomach, shod feet kicking gaily, until he thumps down on the other side and squirms to get as much ground contact as possible.

Over again to the other side. 'Worth a hundred pounds for every time he can roll over,' old horsemen used to say. A horse that is too old or too fat or too stiff to roll over, or who is stupidly trying to do it uphill, will get up and go down again on the other side, but he gets no hundred pounds for that.

My first horse after graduating from the pony, Jenny, who always ran away with me, wearing a driving bit because it was the only one I had, was called Over Again. When I asked why, they said it was because he always went over the jumps. It was a lie, or I was doing something wrong, because soon after I got him, he gave up jumping altogether. He was a champion roller, though, going over and over in ecstasy, even uphill. That was why they had called him Over Again.

When the ritual of rolling is finished, the horse struggles up, plants his feet, stretches his neck, and shakes from head to tail. Dust rises, and settles back again, and most of the mud stays on.

In winter, it's a lost cause to get it all cleaned out of his thick coat.

Console yourself that it may give extra warmth. In a dry summer, the only hope for the dust is to wash it out. Hose him down on a hot day, or go over him with a bucket and big sponge, and scrape the dirty water off with a sweat scraper. Brush his coat when it is dry. Keep him in till then, because if he rolls again while he's wet, you've had it.

If you want to keep your horse clean all the time and still let him satisfy his craving, make a pit of sand or sawdust for him to roll in, as they do in racing stables.

A new horse coming into a stable, or a timid one whom the others bully, may be afraid to get down and roll, because he is so vulnerable with all his feet in the air. The bullies won't even let him get down anyway. They'll come at him with their ears back, if they see him picking an attractive spot. He should be let out on his own first to have his roll in peace, while the others watch, frustrated, kicking the doors.

When they follow him out, the head bully will flop down in the same place, to obliterate the scent of the despised newcomer.

Horses are frightfully snobbish about their social relationships. The hierarchy of the herd is as rigid as it used to be in the days when I was a hospital nurse. If the Junior Probationer answered the telephone to someone wanting to speak to a doctor on his ward rounds, she had to tell the Senior Probationer, who told the Second Year Nurse, who told the Staff Nurse, who told the Ward Sister, who told the doctor, and by the time he got to the telephone, the caller had either rung off or died.

Everybody bullied the next one down the line. The Junior Probationer was the lowest, so she bullied the ward maid, and the maid bullied the patients, who were the lowest of the lot, and helpless.

A new horse joining the group is always disliked, so introduce them to each other gradually. Let the old hands get to know the newcomer as a stable mate, or out on rides, or in an adjoining field, before you turn him out with them. Then stay and watch, because you may have to open the gate for him to escape in a hurry if the others chase him. If he always runs, they'll always chase him. If he stops and kicks out, they will soon leave him alone.

As with human bullies, the best treatment is to bully back. Poor gentlemanly Ben never learned that. He was lonely turned out by himself, but every time I tried him with the others, they would make

him run, dark blue eyes popping with fright, and bite or kick crescent-shaped slices of skin off him if they caught him.

Once when the field gate was open, David chased him into the yard and right into his own loose box and banged the door shut on him with his nose: You stay in your place, you swine.

Some horses never get properly integrated. Like irritating people, they seem to get on the nerves of the others. Ben, who was bought from the race track, was always loathed and despised, although he was the only thoroughbred. Perhaps because of that. We kept him apart and gave him small amiable Oliver who could walk underneath him, which seemed to give them both security.

In any group of horses, one is always boss. Elected by himself or by the others? A bit of both. He announces that he is It, and the others aren't going to argue. He is not necessarily the biggest or the strongest horse, but he is usually the cleverest. So clever that while he maintains the social order of his small herd, he gets a henchman to do his dirty work for him. With the horses I have now, John is boss, but David is the one who does the bullying of inferiors.

The herd instinct is still very strong, even after five thousand years of domestication. It is not a democratic, self-governing herd. It is despotic. Obedience to a leader is bred into every horse. That's why we can train and ride them. A horse's brain is small for the size of its body. Ours is ten times larger in proportion to our size. We dominate a horse by mind over matter. We could never do it by brute strength. Any horse, even a small pony, could kill us easily if he wanted to.

Because of the herd structure, it doesn't work to feed several horses together in a field. You can give each of them a separate grain bucket, but the bossiest one will get more than his share. Hay should be spread out in separate piles, one more pile than there are horses. The boss may waste a lot of good eating time playing a selfish form of musical chairs from one to the other, but the lowest horse will always have a choice of two piles to go to.

Selfish games aren't played in the wild, or roaming on moors or large pastures away from humans, or even in smallish fields when there is no one about; but when the herd is closely involved with people, horses, like dogs, become self-centred and jealous.

They will keep a timid horse from drinking, so give him water before he's turned out. They will stand over the field trough, messing the water about and dribbling pieces of chewed grass into it. They will walk through a pile of hay which another horse is eating, even if they don't want it. They will chase each other away from a visitor with carrots or sugar.

If the visitors don't know much about horses, keep them on the far side of the gate. If you let them into the field with their strange smell and their carrots and their sugar, they may get into the middle of a kicking and biting match, and have to run.

Nancy was an elderly hunter pony, quiet and dependable. But if she was off work that day and off people, she would come at you with her square head low and her teeth bared like a wild beast. Would she have bitten the person with the halter? They never stayed to find out. Even strong men would run shrieking for the fence as if a mad bull were after them.

Puck, the knife grinder's pony, turned into a wonderful beginner's pony. She was dreadfully ugly and common, with a head like a torpedo and knobbly joints, and that awkward twisting action of the hind feet from being over-driven; but she was safe and comfortable and obedient. She could also walk as fast as a horse. One of the worst things about being a child on a quiet pony is that you are always fifty yards behind, or jogging to catch up, and just when you reach the others, they start into a trot.

Puck – she got stuck with a boy's name because the knife grinder called her He and we didn't find out for a month that she was a mare – was unshakeable. You could open umbrellas or let off cap pistols under her nose. She never shied. She led the others past rotating concrete mixers and bonfires and children on tricycles, and across haunted ditches whose muddy water hid the depth. If you fell off – never through her fault – she would stop and wait, nosing you in a motherly way if you were crying. When some sadist plonked you back in the saddle because 'the only thing to do when you fall off is to get right back on again', and trotted on ahead before you could even dry your tears on Puck's moth-eaten mane, she would turn her head from time to time and nudge you with her warty nose to make sure you were all right.

But Puck was Dr Jekyll and Mr Hyde. In the field, she was a monster. She would go on grazing and let you come quite close. Before you could grab her halter, she would either make a snatch at you with her long stained fangs, or whip round and kick out. Her straight little hoofs just reached the hip bone of someone my height.

So we usually caught the others and led them down the road to the stable, and let Puck follow. She would amble down the middle of the narrow lane with a car behind, honking to get by. If it tried to squeeze past her, she'd kick the wing.

Even if your horse is easy to catch, don't get too casual about it, because he will have days – and who shall blame him? – when he doesn't feel like work.

It is better to slide the rope round his neck than to shove the halter straight at his nose. It is better to stand still and call, or give his special whistle and see if he will come to you. If you need food to catch him, take some oats in a bowl or sieve, so that the rattle will attract him.

People are going to tell you that you should not seduce a horse with oats, because it is bribery and you'll never catch him without them. People who tell you that, you'll notice, have horses who are easy to catch.

If yours is not, you will spend a lot of time and energy trying to outwit him. You can't overpower a horse, so you have to outsmart him. Different things work with different horses, and the same one may not work for ever, and if you find a foolproof way to catch a dodgy horse, I wish you'd let me know.

Keep the halter and rope behind your back. If he moves away from you, walk quietly after him. Don't chase him. Don't drive him. Don't get a whole squad of people out to help you herd him into a corner: Mum, Dad, Aunt Mabel, Grandma and the twins, all turning out after Sunday lunch, walking through the wet grass with

their arms out, swishing sticks and going, 'Coop, coop,' or, 'Oy,' or, 'Come hup you devil' at one muddy pony, watching them with a cynical eye. He retreats to a corner, and it serves them right when he breaks out and charges through the end of the line, bowling over Aunt Mabel.

A difficult horse should always wear a halter, with a length of rope – not long enough to tangle him up – which you can grab. What if he won't let you near enough to grab? You keep trying, everything you know, because, like a horse who won't go into a trailer, he may suddenly give up and yield to you.

Even stubborn horses have these sudden surrenders. They get sick of it, or your will power wins.

Usually what happens is that your temper wins. You throw the rope at the horse and go away and miss your ride. We had this speedy dun pony called Titch, and I used to lie in bed when I woke each morning, devising ways to catch him. He was bouncingly fit and lively, and was supposed to be being schooled for a show, but he didn't get ridden enough, because we couldn't often catch him, even in a small field. If we kept him in the stable, his legs swelled like an old lady who has been on her feet too many working years.

When his boy outgrew him and I was going to America, we sold Titch to a woman in Gloucestershire, who had a hard-riding son who wanted a bold fast pony for Hunter Trials, which Titch was very good at, being too tearaway to jump well in the ring. When he came out of the van, they turned him out to stretch his legs, and I heard afterwards that they didn't catch him for three months, and the Hunter Trial season was over.

# Chapter 3

Where I live now, I have the luck to have a fenced yard round the stable, with the field gates leading into the yard. If all the horses are coming in, which they have to on the cold winter nights here, and in the heat of the midsummer days, I put feed in the loose boxes, open the gate, and they come quietly in. If you don't put feed in the mangers, they come straight out again before you can shut all the doors.

A new horse learns his own box very quickly. It smells comfortably of himself. If the bedding is clean, he drops manure right away to make it smell like home. If two horses get into one box by mistake, or on purpose, never go in after them, unless you want your head kicked in. Stand outside and shout and bang on the wall, or poke at them with a broom to get at least one out.

All horses sometimes like to put on an act. They sham lame at the start of a ride. They snort in terror at a white stone going away from home, but don't give it a glance on the way back. They clench their teeth and refuse to take the bit. They swing their head up high if you are a short person with a bridle, but if you are tall with long arms, they don't bother. They won't let you pick up a foot. If you have a back foot in your lap to clean it, they rest their weight on you, as if they couldn't stand a moment longer on three legs.

Showtime would sometimes refuse to come in for his evening feed. Or he would come in, snatch a mouthful, and run out before I could shut the door. Then he would tear round the yard like a maniac, knocking over chickens and loaded wheelbarrows, and dodge back into the field.

He wanted his feed. He was a desperately hungry horse, who would smack his lips and dribble at the mere sound of the lid of the feed bin, but if his loose box was still open, he had a compulsion to come out, to prove it could be done.

I used to try to catch him, because he was well bred and thin coated, and it was too cold for him to stay out. One evening, I got fed up. I was going out, and it was late. I told him to go to the devil, shut up the stable and went in to change. When I came back before I left, Showtime was drooping patiently outside his door as if he were waiting for a bus.

I would like to say that this taught him a lesson and he never played this game with me again; but it isn't so simple with horses. They don't think logically. This horse would still mess about on some evenings, like a child who won't go to bed. If I went indoors and left him, it only meant putting on a coat and boots and gloves later and coming out again after dark.

Showtime was an alcoholic, incidentally. He drank gin and tonic, and he once posed for a beer advertisement, downing a tankard of pale ale.

The horses are in the stable, each with his head in a manger, each standing in his habitual way – along the top wall, diagonally across the box, resting one back foot, leaning on the side wall. If you shove them over, they go back to the same position. They are like old gentlemen in a club who can't digest their steak and kidney if they don't sit at their same table.

It is time to go indoors, but you linger to contemplate the crunchy chewing, the grid of upper teeth moving under the thin skin of the cheek, the hollow above the eye going in and out as the jawbone moves in its socket. It is very satisfying to watch a horse eat.

Nervous horses like to be left alone, but an old chum likes you there, hanging over the door, or leaning on his neck, stroking the loose silk of his chest, watching the gobs of feed run down the long gullet, or steaming your face over the manger in the porridgey warmth of oats and horse breath.

Some horses are impatient if you don't tip the feed immediately into the manger. Some like you to stand slavishly with the bowl while they eat out of it with their head between your arms. They would even like you to hold up the water bucket for them, if you would.

Harvard, a plum-coloured bone-shaker who stayed with me one summer when his people were on holiday nearby, did not drink enough, unless I held up the bucket for him. When I told his owner he should do this at home, he said, 'Sorry, the horse will have to die of thirst.'

They came back next summer with dun Gingerbread. Had Harvard died of thirst? No, the owner had sold him: 'I got tired of holding up the water bucket.'

Barney used to have this phobia about only drinking from the outside trough, never from a bucket. When it was cold enough to drain the trough, his bucket was full of fresh water for two days, three days, but he would not drink, indoors or out. Then someone stood the bucket inside the empty trough, and he drank.

You don't have to be brilliantly clever to cope with a horse. Just cleverer than he is.

If a horse leaves part of his feed, don't leave it in the manger to make him eat it next time, like an old-fashioned mother forcing her child to eat spinach. It never worked with the spinach, and it won't work with a horse.

Give him less food. Take away what he leaves and put it out for the birds and squirrels. Change the feed slightly. Mix in some treacle, cut up apples, carrots. If he eats too fast, put thistles in his food. If he pushes the food out on to the floor, get a manger with an overhanging lip on it. If he eats very slowly, or with his mouth open, dribbling, get the vet. His teeth may need rasping.

If he goes right off his food, noses in the manger and then swings sadly away, turning on you the reproachful eyes of a patient with a gastric ulcer, you may need the vet again. Although a horse can develop neurotic phobias, like Barney with the water trough, a healthy horse will eat. If he goes off his food suddenly, he may be ill, or it may be the onset of colic.

Look at his sides, and feel them. Are they distended like a drum, the skin tight instead of moving loosely over the back ribs? Does he groan? Does he turn his head and look at his stomach, or bump it with his nose? Does he put back his ears and even nip at you? Does he stamp and kick and swing down his head and bang his forehead up against the wall?

Put a rug on him. Warm a blanket in a turned-off oven or on a radiator, and put that under the rug. Keep him standing up, because he could twist his distended intestines if you let him lie down. Take him out and walk him. Wear thick gloves if he is nipping. The friendliest horse gets frenzied with a stomach full of gas.

The vet will give him a colic drench, or a pain-killing or tranquillizing injection. What if there is no vet nearby, or he can't come? Everyone has a different home remedy for colic. My favourite, recommended by a vet, is about a dozen aspirins (less for a pony) crushed in a bottle of some sweet fizzy drink like Coca-cola.

Twelve aspirins, sixty grains, would be a dangerous amount for a person, but is nothing to a horse. It calms the convulsive pains, and so far has worked with Bobby, Flag, Showtime, John, Ben, David and Guy (wind-sucking trouble). Wrap a strip of rag or sticking plaster round the neck of the bottle to protect it from the teeth, get someone to hold up the horse's head, put the bottle in the gap between his front and back teeth, and tip as much of the aspirin and Coca-cola down his throat as you can. A lot of it will go over you.

You can also pour into him three or four cups of ordinary cooking oil, to try to get his intestines working and shift the blockage.

Stay with him. Keep him on his feet. If you have to go into the house, tie him up short so that he can't lie down. If he does, jab him with the bristle end of a broom, tug at him, scare him, use anything, even a whip, to get him up.

An old miner who used to take care of pit ponies underground told me that if they lay down with colic, or just from laziness when they were waiting with a tub full of pit props, he would take his tea bottle and pour a little warm tea in their ear. It got them up at once.

Some horses kick when they are eating, from the excitement of greed, from habit, or from a miserly instinct to scare off marauders. The more they hear their shoes rap and hammer on the side of the box, the better they like it, and the worse the nerves of the poor horse who is trying to eat next door.

Ben practically had the partition between him and David kicked through (revenge for being chased?), until we leaned an innocent broom against it. When he kicked, the broom fell on him, and we laughed.

Some people tie a knotted rope to the tail of a horse who kicks in the stable. Some hang up an old car tyre, slit through so he can't catch his leg in it. When he kicks, it swings back and hits him.

Any punishment you give a horse must come immediately, and it must appear to have been caused by what he did. The horse kicks. The broom or the rope or the tyre hits the part of him that kicked.

If a horse kicks sideways at you when you're grooming him, or doing up a girth or a rug, kick him back on the same leg, so it will seem as if he had kicked himself. Same principle as, if your child bites you, bite it back.

Give feed in a manger, or a tub on the floor, never directly on the floor or on the ground outside, where he could reinfect himself with worms from his own droppings. All horses have a certain amount of worms as permanent residents. You give worm powders twice a year to keep the population under control.

Hay in a rack or a net is neat and not wasteful, but if the hay is a bit dusty or the horse is coughing, wet the hay and put it on the floor, where dust and seeds are less likely to blow into his nose and eyes. If he leaves hay, you are giving him too much. That seems so obvious, and yet some people, especially women and girls, have this sentimental idea that they can express love with food. Mothers stuff gross, unlovable children with cake and puddings to cover their guilt about not loving them enough. Luckily animals are more sensible than gross, unlovable children. A dog will diet himself every so often. A horse might gorge himself to death if he got into the oat bin, but normally he won't eat more than he needs.

31

If the hay is musty, throw it out, or use it as an organic mulch on your vegetable garden. If you use it for bedding, the horse may be perverse enough to eat it, although he has turned up his nose at it in the rack. If giving hay on the floor teaches him to eat his bedding, change the bedding to something like peat or sawdust.

If you have the luck to have a horse, or a friend with one, or a job at a riding stable, you will know that there is muck with the luck, and mucking out is a large part of the work.

If you are a real horse person, you don't care. Mucking out is more fun than housework, and much more needed, because you are doing it for someone who can't do it for himself, whereas the people for whom you sweep and dust and make beds and wash up could usually do it for themselves.

Not that a horse wants his stable cleaned. He likes it dirty. If he comes in to a clean bed, he'll always mess it up. Usually in the

middle where he is going to lie down. Grey or cream horses always do this. Brown ones less often. All the skewbald and piebald horses and ponies I have ever had – Meg, Lollipop, Nancy, Peter, Oliver – always managed to get manure stains only on the white patches.

The greatest brains in the world have given thought to the problem of how a horse could be house-trained, like a dog or cat. It can't be done. Horses in a field will use the same corners, to mark territory and so as not to make all the grass grow rank; but in a stable, only a few of them, mostly stallions, will use the edges, or the same corner.

If you could invent a way to teach a horse to use a trough in a corner of the loose box, you would make your fortune. Or would you?

Dog lovers hate to clean out kennels. Horse lovers like cleaning stables.

A new horse in the stable often won't lie down for a night or two. When you go out in the morning and find bedding on him, you know that he has settled down and accepted this new home.

Horses can sleep standing up, but most of them lie down every night, indoors or out. In books, people go out to the stable where the horse is lying, and sit with his head in their lap and call him Old Pal. In life, it doesn't often work that way. Most horses, unless they are old, or very sure of you, won't be caught lying down.

A horse's natural instinct is to flee from danger. Speed is his only weapon of defence, to run fast with the herd – that's why he can easily be trained for racing. That's why Western breakers will rope a wild colt and throw him off his feet, to confuse and un-nerve him. A horse is always afraid of being caught off guard. Even when he's quietly grazing in his own familiar field, his ears are on the move to pick up warning sounds, and his wide-set eyes can see all round, and behind him through his legs.

This ancient instinct from his primitive wild days is the reason why he will hardly ever let you catch him lying down. If he does, it could mean trouble, like colic or rheumatism, if he has never stayed down like this before.

Bobby would often stay lying down, and drop his nose into my hands as I sat by him. He was too old and stiff to bother to struggle up when I went out to him after dinner, and again at midnight when the cats always come out with me to prowl along the top rail of the fence. Norma, Eileen, Amy, Louise and Lilian, Paul, Dora, Trooper, Tommy, Casey, Doris, Carrie, Nemo – all the cats I have ever had in this house have walked the fences at midnight.

When I had pale Ben, with eyes like big blue-ringed marbles, he would sometimes lie quietly out in the moonlight with his front legs curled under him and his tail fanned out in the grass, and let me sit on his mountainous side.

But he may have been a circus horse at some time during his mild career. I found out by chance one day when I was brushing mud off his legs that when you tapped him below the right knee, he would kneel on it, with his left leg stretched out in front in a bow to the Royal box.

Also, if he had side reins on, you could lunge him with just a whip, no lunge rein. He would canter steadily round, as if a lady in a tutu and spangles were dancing on his back. Sometimes he would canter in front and trot at the back. We imagined that he had been thrown out of the sawdust ring for that worst of circus sins, against which the trainer watches with a flicking whip as the horse learns to canter slower and slower – the 'trot-gallop'. The spangled lady can't dance if the front and back ends are doing different things.

Sometimes after winter, when the sun puts out its first real warmth,

horses will stretch out and bask in the promise of spring. They lie flat out on their sides with their necks stretched and their eyes closed, and people ring up to say they have just gone past the field and that big yellow horse is dead.

Once, when it was poor old Specs stretched out, in the winter, she *was* dead, or dying.

She was over twenty, and had known a hard life in riding schools and summer camps, always in demand because she would canter when you said 'canter', so you didn't have to learn to use your legs (like eager Barney being schooled for a Handy Hunter Pony class, in which he had to stop between two jumps. 'Pull him in as he lands ... get your weight back ... raise your hands ... drop your hands...' Everyone told his child how to do it. She went away to the far side of the course and came back smiling. 'He does it perfectly.' 'What did you do?' 'I said Whoa.').

Poor old Specs was turned out with John, who quite liked the old lady. But when she lay down for her last rest on the frosty ground, he tried to kick her in the head.

Chickens will peck at a sick hen to get rid of her from the flock. The instincts of John's forbears of thousands of years ago told him that the weaker members must be destroyed, so as not to hold back the herd.

# Chapter 4

'Would you like to come and see the horses?'

This is the best treat I can offer a visitor, and it is always a shock to discover that not everybody wants to. Sometimes they politely pretend that horses give them asthma or shingles. Sometimes they just say, 'No thanks.'

But here are three visitors who have agreed. That is, the first has said, 'Oh yes, *please*.' The second has said, 'I don't mind.' The third has said, 'Been mixed up with horses all my life, but I may as well take a look at what you've got here.'

The horses are in the stable, because I am hoping to go for a ride as soon as I can get rid of the visitors. As we cross the drive, I whistle, and call John's name.

Horses learn their own name very quickly. If they are rechristened, the new name soon takes over, although they remember the other one for ever, and will prick an ear to it if an old friend calls.

I call to John, and Barney answers, but I pretend to the visitors, who can't see the horses yet, that it is John.

Going through the tack room, as you do in my place to get to the loose boxes, the first visitor, a young girl, raises her head and expands her nostrils to the intoxicating stable smells, observes what kind of saddles we have, and puts out a hand to touch a bridle on a peg.

The second visitor, a city lady too elegantly dressed for overdone cold beef and baked potatoes in the kitchen, which is what she has had, wears quite a different face. She is wrinkling her nose and blinking her eyes as if she smelled ammonia, which she does, since the mare's stable is always a bog an hour after you clean it.

The husband, 'mixed up with horses all my life', wears no expression on his face. He doesn't seem to smell anything. He doesn't glance at anything in the tack room as we walk through, so I need not have worried whether I could sneak out and give the floor a quick sweep before they came out.

The girl goes quietly up to a horse with her hand held below his nose and stands still while he gets the smell of her. The city lady lets

out a refined squeal as a large palomino head looms over a door at
her, steps back, trips over a cat, and retreats to the top of the mounting block with her arms folded defensively, as if there were mice
about. Her husband strides up to the mare, who is obviously the
shyest from the way her ears flick back and forth, cries, 'Hey there,
you know me, hey, come on, what do you say there, old boy!' in
angry tones. He flings up a hand and the mare flings up her head.

'Don't throw up your hand,' the young girl says gently. 'Hold it
low and let her smell you.'

'Don't worry, they know people who know them.' He flings up
his hand at John, who jerks up his head like the mare. 'Come on,
what's the matter with you?' He grabs at John's nose, and the black
horse retreats to the back of the box.

'Unfriendly devil. Wants a bit of work,' the man says com-
placently. 'If I had the right gear on, I'd give him a go round for
you.'

'Do you ride?' the girl asks politely. He has a big bottom and
short legs.

'My dear girl, ridden all my life.' But you know that if you were rash enough to let him get on a horse, he probably wouldn't even know how to hold the reins.

When people like that say, 'ridden all my life,' it usually means that they have ambled out on a dejected riding school plug, or plodded down the Grand Canyon on a mule, or sat on a farm horse when they were six.

When the man says generously, 'I'll have to come back some day and exercise these nags for you,' I pretend not to hear.

When he repeats it, the girl says, 'They are turned out most of the time, which is better than being ridden by the wrong – I mean strangers.'

'You ride?' he asks her indifferently, blowing cigarette smoke at David.

'A bit.'

David throws back his head and curls up his top lip away from the tobacco smoke.

The lady on the mounting block says, 'Look, he's laughing!'

Her husband throws down his cigarette end. When I go to stamp it out, I whisper to the girl to stay on after they have gone, and ride with us.

Once we had a garden party for a politician who was trying to get elected. He arrived with his wife, very chic in a gorgeous expensive black dress. They were early, so to kill time and avoid having to make political conversation to her, I took her to see the horses.

They had just been fed. Rosie, a deranged thoroughbred who later was sold as a brood mare after she took me sideways into the main road traffic, swung round from the manger and blew damp oats and bran all over the front of the politician's wife's lovely black dress. I thought she would be furious, but she laughed.

It wouldn't brush off, so I sponged it down and made a terrible stain on the silk. Her husband said that she had let him down by not appearing at her best before prospective voters. She didn't mind, because it turned out she liked horses better than politics.

We had a horse called Wallace, a tall grey horse who was a powerful jumper, but very erratic and nervous.

We had to sell him. We advertised, and a woman came to see him who said she wanted a horse to school as an Open Jumper. She didn't seem to know much about horses, though. When we took her out to see Wallace, roaming restlessly round his box with the lining of his rug shredding out where he plucked at it, she pushed out a sudden hand at him, although his ears were back.

A snap. A scream. She clutched her hand and doubled over, and Wallace spat the very tip of her finger on to the floor. We picked it up and jammed it back on and wrapped the hand in towels and dashed her to hospital. The fingertip was sewn in place and healed perfectly; but she was still angry, although it was her fault.

In the stable, you can tell at once whether people know anything about horses or not.

A horse should hear your voice before you make any move. If he is standing back in the box as you approach, speak to him before your head suddenly appears in the doorway. Inside, speak to him before you go up and touch him. It's good to talk to him all the time whatever you are doing. Grooming, tacking up, mucking out round him, a continual innocent prattle is even more pleasing to a horse than the old-fashioned groom's soothing way of hissing through his teeth.

When you go behind him, always speak, and lay a hand on his rump as you go round. If the corner of his eye suddenly sees you when he didn't know you were there, he'll be scared, and when he's scared, he kicks.

If he is a kicker, go round the front end, especially in a stable, where you can get slammed against the wall before you can jump out of the way. When you are brushing his tail, or trimming his heels, or picking out his hind feet, stand as close to him as possible. If he tries to kick, he can only push you. If you stand nervously a few feet away, you are just the right distance for his hoofs.

A horse's sense of smell is very important to him, and must be satisfied. Let him smell anything new. If you go in with liniment or ointment or powder, take the top off and let him sniff at it before you use it on him.

A curious or suspicious horse like John has to smell everything, even something familiar, like a brush that has been used on him hundreds of times. If you go in with some bogey like a clean cloth, and don't give him a chance to check it with his nose, he will snort and tremble and whirl round in circles as if a snake had reared up out of his bedding.

Because John was bred roaming free, he is so terrified of snakes that he has a fit if he hears any hissing. An old-fashioned groom would get nowhere with him. You can't use a fly spray on him, or anything that comes in an aerosol container. Once at a picnic, some-one opened a can of beer near him, and he broke his halter and took off across the countryside as if he had been shot.

When you go to work with brush and curry comb, remember that a horse may be ticklish and sensitive, so go easy on the places where he fusses. If he hates having his face cleaned, even with a sponge or a soft body brush, hold him firmly and do it quickly and gently. If he can't stand having his mane pulled, get one of those thinning combs that have a little blade inside. If he goes berserk when you try to pull his tail, don't make an issue of it. Plait the top of the tail if you take him to a show. It looks just as neat.

Most horses will go well in a snaffle, but a few will chuck it up into the corners of the mouth and yaw about and never get used to it. If he hates a snaffle, stick to a pelham, or whatever he likes. If he hates a curb, and fusses his head up and down, or gets overflexed, stick to the kindly snaffle.

You hear people say through set teeth, 'I won't give up. He's got to learn.' But battling on with something that annoys or scares a horse, won't get him used to it. It will make him worse.

Find a way round it. Be tactful. Be flexible. Be adaptable. Change some fault, then adapt yourself to it. That's usually easier than trying to adapt the horse.

Sometimes you see a horse at a show, going so smoothly and beautifully, making it all look so easy that you are enviously tempted to condemn it as 'a push-button horse'.

But if you were in an equitation class where you had to change horses, you might see how well the rider of that horse had adapted to its faults. It looked foolproof, but *you* can't do a thing with it. If it is a 'push-button horse', you are pushing the wrong button, you realize, as you wear out your outside leg trying to keep it cantering, or tear madly round and round the ring and run over the judge.

If your horse refuses a fairly high jump, put it down a bit. If he keeps running out on the same side, lean a bar on that side for a wing, and remove it when he's got used to taking the jump in the middle. If he cow-kicks when you're tightening the girth, get someone to hold up a front foot. If he is nervy and restless alone in the stable, leave a radio playing, or a ticking clock, or get him a sheep or a goat or a cat. Or another horse.

If he begins to get tense and jumpy as you approach some pet bugbear like a pig farm or a flapping tarpaulin, start chatting to him, or singing to the rhythm of the trot, and keep on with the song until you have passed. The horse will be slightly hypnotized by the song's rhythm, and reluctant to break his stride.

Change the subject. Distract him. Mother chimpanzees have no difficulty with their babies, because when they head for trouble, they say, 'Hey, look at this!' and switch their attention to a banana skin, or an ant, or their own ticklish toes.

Any sort of battle with a horse is always a mistake, unless you are sure that he is being deliberately – what's the word? Naughty is too childish. Evil? A horse has no native evil in him. Wicked? Vicious? Only a real rogue could be called that, and then it has probably been a much wickeder and more vicious human who made him so. Get rid of that one. There are plenty of amiable horses and ponies in the world, and it costs as much to keep a bad one as a good one.

Rebellious is the word, perhaps. A horse may try it on to see what he can get away with. If you think he is being deliberately rebellious, and you must battle it out to remind him who's boss, be sure you can win before you start, and do it where people aren't watching. They will tell you what to do, and what you're doing wrong. They'll perch on the gate and laugh at you. When Dianne's young Olympic rider was charging round the jumps with his strategy of 'over, under or through', the girl next door sat in a tree and cackled like a hen. One day he brought out a water pistol and shot her down as he was crashing through the brush jump.

A horse is not often rebellious. He has inherited too many centuries of obedience to man. Incorrigibly bad horses were not likely to be bred from, and so through generations, the wilder characteristics were gradually weeded out, and the desirable ones developed.

If a horse behaves badly, it's more often from fear or confusion. Fear is very strong in his nature. Most horses are cowards, because their self-preservation instinct is to flee, not fight. Brave horses are either too stupid to see danger, or have developed so much confidence in a human being that they don't look for it.

A horse is easily confused. He may seem to refuse to obey, but perhaps he doesn't know what you want of him. Make sure it's him, not you, and don't blame him for your mistakes.

A well-trained horse gets more easily confused than an unschooled one. Taught to follow certain aids and signals, if he gets the wrong

ones, his world falls apart, especially if he is punished for not obeying the wrong command.

Here's the Sack, for instance, clambering up on a nice willing horse. She heaves her bulk into the saddle by the reins, not by the neck, or the mane. She tries to turn him from a standstill. He can't do that any more than a car can, however hard you turn the wheels.

'Get on.' She kicks him forward without easing her hands forward. He moves readily and gets a jab in the mouth. His eyes are worried already.

Having trotted round the ring with a humped back, rising too high, and thumping down, heels swinging into the horse behind the girth, hands hard on his mouth when this makes him move faster, she decides to risk a canter.

He has been taught to canter by the rider sitting down in the saddle and using the outside leg. So has the Sack, but genuine sacks know better, and ride round with their hard hats jammed over their ears, deaf to instruction. She leans her lumpish weight forward and goes click-click. What's this? The horse has no idea what she wants, so he trots faster, and gets stopped with a tug on his mouth. She tries again. Same result. And again. Same result, including a stumble, because she has turned his head so far to the rail that he can't see where he's going. Once when he does hopefully swing into the canter stride, her hands aren't ready for him, and he gets it in the mouth again. His ears go back. The Sack is fussed too.

'Sit back a bit!' someone calls.

'It's this stupid horse.'

'Keep his head up!' But she has never listened to advice yet, especially from someone younger, so the horse gets his head down and bucks, and the Sack flops off like a bag of garbage falling from a third-floor window.

You are not the Sack, or you wouldn't be reading this book, since sacks are only interested in horses as vehicles, or something to boast about at school; but we all confuse our horses some of the time. They don't understand us, and we don't understand them.

Rebellion? Fear? Confusion? If you can find out *why* your horse does what he does, you are half-way to knowing how to cope with it.

If you can understand your horse as a horse, not as a rather slow-witted brand of human being with four legs and a tail, you will be able to treat him like a horse, which is what he needs.

Seeing animals in terms of people, and crediting them with human emotions and feelings and reactions they cannot possibly have, is called anthropomorphization.

People praise a dog for being 'almost human'. What kind of praise is that? A dog is a dog. That's the best thing about him. If we develop a close relationship with a dog, we don't say that we are 'almost canine'.

Horses get anthropomorphized. People say things like, 'He understands everything I tell him.' He doesn't, of course, any more than a dog does. He can recognize certain key words, like his name and simple commands, but the rest is tone of voice.

If you stroke his neck and say lovingly, 'You're a foul, ugly brute and I hate you and I'm going to get a whip and beat you till you can't stand,' he will bend his ear and eye to you with a calm pleasure.

If you fling up an arm and growl savagely, 'I love you, you're strong and swift and the most beautiful horse in the world!' he'll throw up his head and jump back, rolling his eye and trembling.

Understands everything you tell him? Since we are more intelligent than horses, it would make more sense for us to understand what they are telling us. If people ever really learn to talk to horses, it will have to be in their language, not ours.

And it will have to be quietly.

'Come up, you brute! Get over there! Stand still, damn you!' A horse gets yelled at as if he were a dangerous criminal.

'Whoa! Whoa, Travell-aa-aa!' A child on a too hot pony shrieks like a train whistle, and Traveller travels faster.

Yelling doesn't make a horse obey. It makes him scared. Horses are very sensitive to loud noises, which is why they generally like women better than men. Women's voices are quieter, or are supposed to be. I've known some deafening female trainers and riding teachers and horsey mothers.

'Legs, Amanda, legs I said, dammit – get that brute moving!'

'Pick 'em up there, you clumsy devil! Push him on – impulsion!' A leathery woman who goes to the small shows round here sets up a practice jump behind her trailer, and beats white-faced children over it with curses and a whip.

Being a horse maniac is one thing. Being crudely horsey is another. Horses should improve people and make them more sensitive, not coarsen and spoil them.

One of the most embarrassing sights is a female of any age losing her temper in public. You don't see it at the better shows, but at smaller local ones, you still sometimes do.

The horse refuses for the second time, and this person lays about him with a whip, jerking on his mouth, whip going both sides, red in the face.

Three refusals. The horn tootles, or the ring steward says, 'Thank you' (for nothing), and she rides out of the ring scarlet and panting, her mouth like an iron bar and her hands like lead.

Occasionally it's a child who rides out in a rage, jumps off, flings the reins at Mum with, 'This rotten pony's no good,' and stamps off to the ice cream van. Last summer, I heard a brat in pigtails complain, 'This rotten whip's no good,' as she flung it at her mother.

One of the times when you do need a whip is if your horse develops the loutish habit of trying to push his way out of the stable as soon as you open the door.

If he is constantly shoving at his door, and kicking it with his

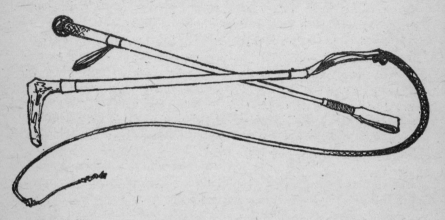

front feet, you can fix a bar across the open top part, so that he can't get his head over to push with his chest, and hang a sack full of something prickly like gorse where he kicks.

If he is always trying to push past you, go in next time with a whip. Say, 'Get back,' very firmly, and give him one across the chest. Once is usually enough. After that, if he starts shoving again, bang the whip against the outside of the door. Go in and just tap him with it, repeating, 'Get back'. You may not even have to touch him. Just waggling the whip at him will send him discreetly back. After that, just, 'Get back' will do it.

Whips should be handled with caution, like guns. They are often made in a dangerous way, with a piece of thick wire down the middle, so always check an old one to make sure the leather padding on the end is not worn away, and the sharp metal exposed.

At a riding stable, a very pushy horse was kept in a narrow stall. It was hard to get by him to the manger, as he would crowd you against the partition. The girl who worked there got tired of being pushed and stepped on, so she took a whip in with her to keep the horse over.

He crowded her, as usual, and somehow she jabbed the whip at him in such a way that the metal end went right through his side between his ribs and into his lung.

The poor girl would gladly have had every one of her toes trodden black and blue, rather than that tragedy.

It is usually people's own fault when they get stepped on, but it's no use telling them that, when they are standing there yelling in agony, trying to push a ton weight of horse off their toe.

Horses hate to step on anything soft and squashy, and will usually avoid you if you fall, but when they step on your toe, they stand there dreamily, and it practically takes dynamite to get them off.

Don't go into the stable with bare feet (there is a risk of tetanus too, if you have a cut or scratch). Watch where you put your feet, and where the horse puts his. But when it happens, and it will, remember, in your agony, that the trademark of a horse keeper is at least one permanently blue big-toe nail.

# Chapter 5

If you ride a bicycle, you can get on, ride it, jump off again, and not even put it away if you don't want to, just chuck it down with the wheels spinning.

If you ride a horse, you can't just get on it and ride and get off again. It takes time to get ready, and time to take care of everything when you come back. The take-it-or-leave-it people think this is an awful bore. They hang about in the house in the hope that someone else will get their horse ready. When they come back, they make some excuse, like a telephone call, or something in the oven, to go indoors before the work is finished.

But to horse people, the preparations and the work that go with riding are half the charm. Sailors feel the same about their boats. Car enthusiasts spend almost as much time lying under the car or with their head inside the engine as they do in the driver's seat.

With horses, what you do when you're out of the saddle matters just as much as what you do when you're in it. It's all part of the same fascinating ritual.

Even though you are going to ride alone, you don't feel right unless you start out on a clean horse. If he stayed in last night, you have groomed him this morning. If he's in the field, you bring him in and get the mud off him. Take out his water bucket so that dust doesn't settle on it. Always take the water out if you're using a fly spray, or you'll get an oily chemical film on top.

Talking of buckets, be sure that the handle is down flat. A thirsty horse might paw at an empty bucket, and get his foot caught in the handle. He might not break a leg, but he will certainly smash the bucket.

Think ahead, and prevent things before they happen. Hammer in a sticking-out nail. I've seen a horse with half the side of its neck ripped away from one nail in the wall. Don't leave rakes or forks in the stable, or anything like gloves or a halter or bridle that he can chew. He will. Everybody knows not to leave forks and rakes with the prongs sticking up. Or do they? There are still accidents. Hang up your pitchfork, or stick it into a bale of hay.

If the horse is very dirty, tie him up to clean him outside, so that the dust blows away, especially if you are prone to hay fever, or if you have just washed your hair. Horse keepers need to wash their hair more often than most people. They also need to keep special clothes and boots for the stable. You may like the smell of horses on you all the time, but other people in your house may not.

You brush out his mane and tail, pick out his hoofs, and oil them if you are feeling thorough. He's ready. The stimulation of the

grooming makes him feel vigorous. Since he is a creature of habit, he knows that the bridle follows; but he may be one of those clowns who, even if they enjoy being ridden out, go round and round the box presenting you with the threat of the back end. If you know he never kicks – or if you don't know, but are braver than me – you march right up alongside him. If he can turn quicker than you can get to his head, keep his halter on after grooming, and leave him tied up while you fetch the bridle.

Most horses take the bit quite happily if they have been properly handled, but some are difficult, either through rough treatment, or being allowed to get away with evasive tactics.

David, who is over sixteen hands, used to belong to a short man who had to stand on a box to bridle him. He had the habit of throwing his head up high, craning his long giraffe neck, nose knocking down the strip of sticky fly paper. Being tall with long arms like an ape, I was able to get the hand holding the top of the bridle on to the poll between his ears, and lean on it. There we would stand, me pressing downward and David pushing upward, until he sighed and dropped his head. This has worked so well that now when you start to put on the bridle, he drops his head so low that you almost have to kneel on the floor to get the bit in.

Ben was officially called Loch Raven, and had his thoroughbred number tattooed inside his top lip, although one figure was blurred, as if it had been tampered with.

That may have been why he was taken out of steeplechasing. Or perhaps it was because he dropped his legs from the knee and ploughed through jumps like a hay rake.

When we first went to try him, he was in a dark corner box in a large stable. The man brought him out for inspection, with the usual commentary of, 'Go all the way for you ... heart's as good as his bone ... very typey horse,' and other such occult pronouncements with which horse traders attempt to confuse the real issue, which is that the asking price is too high.

'Make a nice lady's hack,' or hunter, according to which you are looking for. 'Bred to carry a man,' if you happen to be a man. 'Just get in under the stick,' if you are a child looking for a 14.2 pony.

After we had stood about and chewed hay and sucked our teeth for a while, and run knowledgeable hands down Loch Raven's legs, we asked if we might try him. This suggestion is always greeted with surprise, as if the mere sight of the horse should be enough to make you reach for your cheque book.

'Try him? Well yes, you could *try* him, I daresay,' looking at your boots to see if they are worthy. 'Throw a saddle on him, Betsy.'

Betsy took another stable girl into the dark corner box, and the man engaged us in conversation about the horses we could have seen if we had come yesterday, while Loch Raven was being tacked up, which took a long time.

When we got him home and he was Ben, we found out why. It was almost impossible to get a bridle on him. Snaffle, pelham, rubber – mouth kimberwicke – he clamped his teeth tightly shut, and even fingers in the mouth both sides, even a fingernail in the gum would not make him unclench them.

His problem was that his back teeth were jagged and tender, and he was afraid of a bit being pulled roughly up against them. The vet came and filed them, after a double dose of tranquillizer which left Ben leaning groggily against the wall, but still fighting. He still clenched his teeth, because a horse's habits are quickly learned and slowly lost. When I was alone and in a hurry, I could usually get in the bit by holding sugar with it, and slipping it in with the sugar. One Sunday, I had no sugar, no carrots, and a handful of oats wouldn't do it.

Eventually I learned that if your right hand held the bridle at the front of his head instead of at the top, and pinched his nose so tightly that he snorted, he had to open his mouth, and your left hand slipped in the bit.

Gradually, as his unimaginative brain began to realize that it didn't hurt, he became easier to bridle, although he still occasionally cemented his teeth together, always when you were in a hurry.

Ben was a galloping machine. If you gave him his head on an open stretch or an empty beach, he would go off at forty miles an hour, the most exhilarating thrill in the world, the nearest thing to flying.

His limbs were speedy, but his mind was slow. Most horses have a good sense of direction, even in a strange countryside. They have a built-in compass which tells them, not where North is, but where home is. Ben never knew, even on familiar ground. If you dropped the reins at a crossing, he always picked the wrong way. You had to steer him round bushes and trees. Once, when his rider was not looking, Ben ran himself into a telegraph pole.

When I was riding him over the crossroads in the middle of the village, a car slowed to let us pass, but continued to roll slowly forward. It rolled right into Ben, who kept on walking, even after it gently bumped him. The car door opened and a stricken old man got out.

'What did I hit?'

'A horse.'

'Don't tell the police. I'm blind in one eye and the other is going.' He got back in the car and drove off. Ben walked on, his navy blue eye dreaming.

'Throw a saddle on him, Betsy' is not the way to put on a saddle, as everyone knows, except film cowboys who stand back and hurl a heavy Western saddle on to a small quarter horse.

You put the saddle on gently, well forward, so that the hair lies down as you pull it back. If you are the kind of person whose life is dedicated to achieving the most with the least expense of time and energy, and whose staircase is littered with items waiting for the next time someone goes up, you will put on the saddle from the off side. You've got to check under the flap anyway to see that nothing is twisted, so it's simpler to start there than to start on the near side, walk round to the off, and back to the near side to do up the girth.

If the horse, not being as stupid as we think, blows himself out so that the girth can't be too tight, pull it up gently and tighten it later. Always check it before you get on. If he has blown out, he will let go air as he walks outside, and you will end up underneath his stomach as the saddle slips round.

I knew a girl – I always seem to know someone to fit all disasters, but it's true, it has all happened to me – a girl who didn't check the girth on Dynamite, and she put out her hand as she fell, and broke her arm falling off at a standstill.

Make your horse stand while you get on. It may be pleasantly casual to swing your leg over his back as he moves ahead, but when a tree takes your hat, or you drop your gloves or your lunch on a narrow woodland path, you'll be glad of a horse who stands still while you get off and on.

If he wheels round away from you, tighten the right rein. If he still wheels, while you hop after him with one foot in the stirrup, take the foot out and stand in front of him until he stands still, or get someone to hold him while you mount, until he learns.

If a group is going out, everybody waits for the last person. No horse will stand still if the others are moving out of the gate. Once up, fiddle a bit with stirrups, girths, reins, to get him used to standing until you give him the signal to walk on.

But don't fiddle interminably, or no one will go riding with you. Think of everything you need – hat, gloves, sugar, whip, handkerchief if it's nosey weather – before you get up, not after. Forgetful people are always on the tallest horse, and trying to con someone else into getting off and fetching things.

Adjust your stirrup length without making everyone wait while you alter it up and down, and forget which hole it was in, and ask people to look at you from the front to see if your feet are level.

If the length isn't right after you have settled down in the saddle, alter the stirrups as you go along. Don't make everybody stop in the middle of traffic while you fiddle some more.

Once I took a woman riding because I was sorry for her, since she was always so depressed. She could ride fairly well, but she would not settle down and just ride. Every few yards, her stirrups must be altered, and that took her so long that I finally got off and did them for her. She liked that. We had only trotted on a hundred yards before she called out to stop. Her right stirrup was too long.

'Sit straight in the saddle,' I suggested, since that was the trouble.
'How can I, with uneven stirrups?'

It was a rotten ride. She wanted to trot 'for exercise' – and God knows her figure needed it – but as soon as we got going, she would shout to pull up. Stirrups again, or she was out of breath, or had a stitch, or the horse was pulling, or stumbling, or she had dropped something, or thought she saw a deadly nightshade. Finally she dropped her glasses, and since she couldn't see to look for them without them, I had to get off and search the undergrowth.

I gave her Bobby to hold while I hunted, and she let him go. He moved off, picked up speed as I moved after him, and trotted off home with his leg through his reins and his stirrups flying.

We rode home double on Wendy. She had the saddle and I sat behind on the spine. Bobby was in the stable yard. When I asked her whether she wanted to start out again, she said No thank you, she wasn't used to rides where so many things went wrong, but I could go back and look for her glasses if I liked.

Why did I take her in the first place? Feeling sorry for someone is not enough reason to share your treasure. Riding is such a unique and tremendous joy that it's a crime to waste it on anyone who doesn't appreciate it. Let them hire or buy a horse and grumble out on that for exercise. They are not going to do it on mine.

# Chapter 6

So many horses, so many rides, so many hours and hours of true pleasure, never to be forgotten.

Riding is a completed joy, so full of promises fulfilled. There is never a totally 'bad ride'. There are days when you ride badly, or the horse doesn't go so well, but there is always something to find out. Nothing stands still. You never know it all. You learn something each time, even if it's only that you are not as good as you thought you were. The truth about riding is always there for you to discover all over again: if you do it right, it works.

Riding is freedom. There is a girl whose parents are rich and unhappy (the two don't need to go together, as we like to think), and they depend too much on her to give some purpose to their idle, squabbling life. They use her. They are very demanding. They drag her into their boredom and complaints, and she suffers it, in a dead sort of way, until she can escape to the stable. She never smiles, except when she is on her horse.

She told me, 'If I couldn't ride, I'd go insane. When I ride, I'm free.'

If a car passes me when I'm on a horse, I always think: if I were in that car and saw me, I would wish I was me.

Wistful children's faces, staring out of the back window, agree.

In Oxfordshire, where I had Chips, Meg, Jenny, Over, Tonia and others, there was a duckpond outside the house. Meg, bought young from gipsies and never properly broken, used to walk into it and lie ponderously down like an old lady taking a bath.

The child who rides her isn't very strong, so someone grabs her rein and pulls her past the pond, as we start out early on a Sunday morning to make the most of the treasured weekend, that will end this afternoon with dumb misery on the way home, and tears into the soup at supper.

I am about eleven or twelve. I am riding the mealy brown pony Jenny in the driving bit, a straight bar with two rings each side, one sewn to the cheek strap, one to the rein. Jenny, Jemma, Robert and

Meg, we trot along the grass verge of the road, hopping over or stumbling into the drain ditches, and turn into a chalky lane known as Wormcast, since this is one of the places where Saint George confronted his giant worm, the dragon.

We canter single file between the deep cart ruts. There is an iron pot in the hedge that Jenny always shies at. I have given up stopping to let her inspect it, because she would rather shy at it. Meg falls behind. She is rather slow, because she's young and unawakened, but her child likes it that way, because she can relax and sing sad hymns. When I let her ride Jenny once, she started to chant, '*There is a green hill far away*' with a loose rein, and was round a corner and out of sight before she got to '*a city wall*'.

We pull up and wait for Meg at the gravel pit with the precipice over which bold, drunken Sir Somebody is said to have galloped to his death, and may still sometimes be seen, headless on a headless horse, plunging over the edge into nothingness.

And still of a winter's night, they say,
  when the wind is in the trees,
When the moon is a ghostly galleon
  tossed upon cloudy seas.

That's a good one to recite as you trot.

When the road is a ribbon of moonlight
  over the purple moor . . .

Meg arrives, and we turn up a grass path between fields, cantering collectedly in pairs, pretending we are the army. I always think, on the way out, that perhaps I was wrong about Jenny, or that I have finally learned how to ride her, or that she has taken a turn to reform. She doesn't pull at the start, and I think she's not going to, but then we gallop, or we turn the corner that is the farthest point from home, and I change my mind.

At the top of the path, we turn on to the chalky, turfy track that is said to have run right across England in prehistoric days. The Saxons named it the Icknield Way. It runs below these Chiltern hills, crosses roads, divides fields, skirts the edges of woods, curves round steep slopes. No one may build on it or fence it off or plough it up, or do anything but walk or ride on it, from Britwell Salome, where I spent the best of my childhood, all the way to Princes Risborough and beyond.

Sometimes it narrows to a single track between banks grey with the silverleaf fern. Sometimes it widens out so you can ride four abreast. Jenny jogs slightly ahead, wet on the shoulders and neck already. Jemma walks fast with her thick tail swinging like a bell. Robert is frothing for nothing. He doesn't pull or fuss, but he manufactures froth like toothpaste, his crested sea horse mane and the long red hair of the girl who rides him blowing away from the wind. Meg has woken up a bit. Her child has picked an elderberry stick to keep her spirits up.

For a short stretch, the Icknield Way is a flinty lane, past the house where a poet lives, in a romantically tangled garden where roses strangle the trees and the windows are half-blinded with creeper; past the charred ruin from which the derelict old woman was taken by firemen to the cottage hospital, where she now reposes, curiously clean and bright-eyed.

We cross the main road, under the chalk arrowhead cut out on the slope of Watlington hill long before the Romans came, and the next stretch is wide and green and smooth, like a race-course.

Here it runs close to the little branch line between Watlington and Princes Risborough. There is a train leaving the station behind us. We wait until it is level. Jenny stands on her back legs for a moment, then plunges into the bit and we go, wind whistling, train whistling for the Shirburn crossing, driver grinning, people in the two carriages going to do their Sunday visiting waving out of the windows.

Jemma, who started ahead because she doesn't waste time standing on her back legs, throws splatters of mud into my face. But she's not so fast since she had her daughter, Tonia. I pull out to pass her.

Jenny runs like a rabbit, ears back, head parallel with the ground, narrow hoofs reaching far ahead. She is neck and neck with Jemma and the train. She draws ahead – no one can catch her! She's only thirteen two, and bred heaven knows how – we got her at a sale – but she's as fast as a polo pony, and her joy is to gallop.

The train pulls ahead, and the people's faces and arms disappear, while the driver leans far out to give us the thumbs up. His name is Arthur Brewster. He stops at Lewknor Halt to take on Mrs Mumford, who is going to Kingston Blount to see her daughter who is married to a man in the cement factory.

He waits until I canter up and call to him, 'How fast?'

'Fifty!' He is still grinning, but he always grins because his teeth are too big.

'No, honestly.'

'At least thirty then.'

Thirty miles an hour. 'Jenny can go thirty.' I turn round.

'So can Jemma.'

But she was behind. Robert is as fast as Jenny on a short stretch, but his wind isn't good – that's how we got such a spectacular horse

– and the red-haired girl has pulled him up when he began to blow. She jogs up, covered in foam and mud, the big brown horse squandering energy by stepping high. Meg is a brown and white patch in the distance. She plods up, not out of breath, puts her head down to the grass at once, and the child, who is the smallest, falls gently off.

Because of the train passengers, she pretends she got off on purpose. She sits on a stone and takes out chocolate.

The train sighs, pants and starts. Jenny shies at it automatically, although she doesn't mind it. She jogs and fusses and pulls now, because she has galloped at thirty miles an hour, and I change my mind about her being reformed. At the blind corner by the white house, a dog always runs out of the hedge. I tense, knowing Jenny will shy, but the dog runs out barking and she pays no attention, because she never shies at what you expect. A few yards further on, trotting quietly, she has a sudden fit at a small puddle, and takes a devastating leap sideways. Luckily she keeps her head up when she does this, or I would fall off every time.

I get back into the saddle from her firm neck. It is a slightly ewe neck, her worst point. Later when I have saved up for a short-cheeked pelham, I can make her flex so it doesn't show.

We turn off the Icknield Way, up a long fold through sheep meadows dotted with small firs that takes us to the top of the hills. Jenny starts in a galloping bound, then canters, trots, and finally even she walks up the last steep stretch with her head poked forward and her muscles straining.

At the top, we all get off and sit on the crisp turf with the reins over our arms, and stare out at the fields of Oxfordshire, patched with the colours of spring, the young corn greener than the grass. Meg's child has got off half-way up the hill, and they climb dreamily together, propping each other up. At the top, the child lets the pony wander loose. Meg won't go away, but she puts down her head and the reins slip over her neck, and she treads on them, and jerks up her head and breaks the buckle end.

'You'll have to hold one in each hand and remember not to drop them.' But as we ride on, the child forgets, and is seen lying along Meg's neck fishing for the dangling rein, while the skewbald pony goes in circles because she is pulling the other rein.

We trot back along the top of the breezy Chilterns, with the familiar view coming and going between clumps of trees. At Christmas Common, we canter over the squelchy land among darting rabbits, hopping the gorse bushes, and stop at the pub at the end where the wild common suddenly turns into civilized village gardens with pansies and bird baths.

The Red Lion has draught cider, very bitter, which you can drink out of beer tankards, and twopenny packets of square biscuits with a piece of Cheddar cheese.

Now the way is through damp woods where the sun never gets through, and the leaves are thick on the paths, as if it was always autumn.

Which way? There are countless forks and crossings. Jemma walks ahead and chooses, always right, even pushing a short cut through the underbrush where the path takes a wide loop.

Down into a cool hollow, across a shallow stream where everybody drinks but Meg.

'She can't drink through this rubber bit.' Her child takes off the bridle.

'Don't take off the bridle.'

'The reins are round her neck.'

'They're broken, she'll—'

Too late. The reins slip down. Meg, who doesn't want a drink anyway, wanders off, eating curly bracken fronds.

'Don't worry.' She is easily caught. Meg and her child are the sort of people who do everything wrong and get away with it. I am always imagining likely disasters – falling off, foot in rabbit hole, ditch on far side of fence, Jenny shying, stopping dead at a jump, running into wire, car back-firing, man with gun will shoot. Meg and her child take life as it comes, very easy to them both.

Along the far edge of the wood, there are fallen trees to jump. Jemma hops neatly. Robert flies like a Lippizaner doing the *courbette*, head up, all four feet in the air. Meg jumps in two halves, front end over, back end carefully following. If the log is too big, she stops and scrambles over, or finds a way round through the trees. Jenny pulls so hard waiting for her turn that by the time I let go, she is too excited to look at the jump, gets under it and has to buck over.

I take her ahead, and she jumps three big trees in a row like a steeplechaser, sails over the hurdles out of the wood and takes off half-way round the cow pasture before I can turn her and stop.

We cross the tarmac at the top of Howe hill, then canter on the wide grass verge of the gravel road that leads to our own hill, Britwell hill, with the village in a Sunday siesta below. By Coates Farm, we turn through a muddy gateway and go down through the fields alongside the steep hill road.

There is a cut-and-laid hedge at the bottom, not high, but solid, with a slight drop on the far side before the slope up to the road. You can either jump it or go through the gate. The last three or four times, I've made excuses: Jenny too tired, me too tired, ground too wet, ground too hard. Today, Jenny has fussed all down the hill, sideways in a jogging dance. We've ridden for over two hours and my arms and legs are like cooked spaghetti, poor weekend rider that I am, softened by five days at a school desk. Can I go through the gate again without losing face?

Too late. Jemma and Robert are already going at the hedge side by side. They disappear into the drop for a moment, then canter up the slope to the road. I have to let Jenny go. She goes anyway. I grab a handful of mane. She pricks her small curved ears, judges her stride, takes off exactly right, stretches out over the drop on to the far slope and lands cantering. It was perfect.

'Did you see?' No one saw. But it was perfect. If I never jump again, if I die now, if the world ends . . . it was perfect.

Meg comes through the gate, shuts it with her chest, and we walk home along the shallow switchback road into the village, reins loose, not talking. There is no need to talk.

We may not know, we can not tell
what pains he had to bear . . .

Behind us, Meg walks into the duckpond and drinks, muddy water fountaining out from the sides of the rubber bit.

She splashes. 'Get her head up!' The ducks swim apart in arrowheads of alarm as Meg shakes herself all over and flounders out of the pond.

After the horses and ponies are fed, we turn them out before we go back to London. The field is down a narrow sunken lane where beech tree roots grope at the washed-out banks. We ride down bareback with halters, and stay a long time at the gate to watch the horses roll, shake, and wander off, tearing at the grass as if that were their only business in life.

I stare and stare at Jenny. How will she manage all week without me? Just like this, head down to the grass. Perhaps her brain is not capable of thinking of me until she sees me, while mine will have her in it all the time, remembering yesterday's ride to the river at Benson, today's ride with the gallop by the train, and the hills and the woods and the perfect jump, spinning fantasies of great heroism for her and me on the edge of sleep.

Dusk is all round us. The light has gone out of the sky. As we wander back up the lane, kicking pebbles, a grown-up is coming to hurry us up.

'The car's here. It's time to go and you've not even changed.'

'I'll go like this.'

But the shabby, Jenny-fragrant jodhpurs are supposed to stay here, not reek up the car on the way home, and get forgotten next

Friday when we are picked up straight from school after lunch – cod in batter, macaroni cheese, bread-and-butter pudding with the week's stale bread and the custard curdled.

Five days. In the small white bedroom where we keep the fire going all night when it's cold, I leave the things of horses, the jodhpurs, the yellow pullover, the muddy boots, and put on the gym tunic I came down in. It smells of serge and netballs.

Five days. A whole week of school before I can begin to live again next Friday.

# Chapter 7

Arthur Brewster and the train have gone, but you can still ride along the Icknield Way, although there are more cars on the lane that leads there, and you have to wait for traffic on the roads that cross it.

Wherever your riding is, you are almost sure to be on roads some of the way. A horse who is nervous in traffic is a dangerous nuisance.

An inexperienced horse could be turned out in a field near a road to get used to traffic. One of my fields in America has roads on both sides and the fire station at the corner. It lets out a deafening blast at noon and four-thirty, and a fanfare like the crack of doom, if Mrs Riley has a grease fire in her stove, to summon the amateur firemen from workbench and ladder and garage and bank and grocery. If you are passing the fire station on a new horse when the hooter goes off, you'll come home quicker than you wanted; but after he's been out in the field for a week, he won't even lift his head.

A traffic-shy horse could be taken out with a veteran who won't turn a hair if a rattling juggernaut goes by, flapping a tarpaulin and pulling a trailer full of clanging metal. You could lead him out on the road on foot before you try to ride him there. Hold him in your own drive while someone revs up the car, and drives back and forth quite close to him. If he remains nervous and jumpy and unpredictable, like Rosie who used to plunge out sideways in front of lorries, it might be better not to keep him.

It is always difficult to decide how long to struggle on with a problem horse, and when to give up and get rid of him. I hated losing Rosie, who had a fine thoroughbred skin and a canter like silk – unlike her counterpart Rudy, who was popularly supposed to have five legs, even though he was named for a ballet dancer – but after she had gone and we could ride anywhere again without avoiding main roads, I thought how stupid I had been to hang on to her so long.

Yet I have had days when I've gone to bed writing in my head the sale advertisement for a 'hopeless' horse, and tried him again the next day and thought how stupid I was to think of getting rid of him. It was me who was hopeless, not the horse.

In theory, and in the words of the Highway Code, a horse has the right of way, but by the time you shout that to a barbarian driver, you could be dead.

A motorist is supposed to watch out for horses. Too often he assumes that you have a horse out on the road because he is traffic proof, not because this is the only way to get to your riding. He swishes by, much too close, sounding his horn just by the horse's ear. Perhaps he knows you, or would like to know you, or perhaps the sight of you and the horse stirs him to make some kind of noise before he is gone, leaving you jittering in his wake.

If it is a car full of boys, you may get, 'Ride 'im cowboy!' or, 'Hi ho, Silver!' or other old-fashioned and unsuitable greetings, while cigarette ends and peanuts sail out of the window.

Cars are all right when you are in one, but when you are riding a horse along the edge of a busy road, you hate their speed and noise and smell.

Last summer, I took Barney to a show with a pony mare he liked, and when I tried to take him home without her, he went berserk in the trailer.

He called frantically to the mare. He kicked and plunged. He broke the front bar on one side, and when we moved the other one over, he reared up onto it, broke it, and charged out through the small side door, skinning both his hips.

He really is a very quiet pony.

I couldn't get him back into that trailer or anyone else's, so I had to lead him home, five miles along a main road on a Sunday evening, with what seemed like the whole population of New England returning from a weekend on Cape Cod.

It was a two lane road with a narrow stony verge. When cars passed each other abreast of me, there was only just room. Barney, totally unstrung by his affray in the trailer, saw things in the hedge and sidestepped, pushing me into the traffic. I was wearing sandals with wooden soles. As my heel came up, he would step on the sole and nearly break my foot.

People in the cars hooted and waved and called out things, both rude and encouraging. I didn't look to see if I knew them. I hated

them all. The petrol vapour on this road enclosed by high hedges and trees made my stomach sick. The litter I walked on – beer cans, paper cups, chocolate paper, ice cream tubs, broken toys, hub caps, newspapers, plastic bags – made my heart sick.

For some time after that, I kept meeting people who said, 'We saw you walking along the main road with a horse. What on earth were you doing?'

What on earth. Horses and cars don't belong in the same world.

Most drivers, however, are fairly considerate of horses, and riders should always thank them for waiting, or they may not wait next time. Most horses have seen and heard enough traffic not to mind it. They are much less afraid of a car or a lorry than something like a tot on a tricycle, close to the ground, a small person moving on small squeaky wheels.

Small children also like to run behind the horse shouting, 'What's his name?' and, 'Give us a ride, then!'

'Don't run behind the horse,' you warn, but they keep coming, joined by a boy on a bicycle with a playing card fixed to rattle in the front spokes, and a little girl who runs alongside your stirrup, looking up at you with great hankering eyes, and panting, 'I like your horse.'

'May I pat him?' Children always want to pat and stroke. All human beings want to fondle an animal. Psychologists say that this is because we have all grown too remote from each other, and don't hug and cuddle after babyhood, so we fill this need with animals.

Most horses don't mind dogs, because most stables have a dog of their own. Unless a strange dog jumps out suddenly, they don't worry if it runs at them, and won't kick, even if it nips at their heels. When I had the dog Roger, he was always in fights, self-started because a dog came too near his horse, or started by the other dog because Roger went too near his property. The fights would start up right under Guy's heels, and although he was a nervous horse, he never turned a hair. I could even ride him into the middle of a bad fight to stop it, like a police horse quelling a riot.

When a horse shies at a barking dog, rampaging back and forth on its lawn like the last defender of the castle, it is sometimes because the rider is afraid it will shy at the dog, and transmits the fear. Sometimes, like Jenny, who never shied at what I expected, a horse only shies at what you don't see.

Sometimes you don't see it because it isn't there.

Do horses see ghosts? There are old legends about 'Hard-to-come-by' corners that horses refuse to pass, because someone once hanged himself there, or some other ancient tragedy haunts that spot.

A horse also remembers a place where he was once frightened. There is a certain harmless patch of long grass round which John will always make a detour, bulging his eyes and snorting. A frog jumped there four years ago. He has never forgotten.

No other animal, even the timid deer, shies like a horse shies. This is because of the instinct to look out for danger and run (eohippus ran on his toes, which is how the longest middle one developed into a hoof, while the others disappeared into what are now the tiny splint bones). It is also because of the way his eyesight works. He is almost certainly colour blind, and a white object like a sheet of paper is a surprise in his shades-of-grey landscape.

I did an experiment with different coloured bowls, feeding each horse out of the same bowl for a long time. Then I put the four bowls in the yard, and let each horse out in turn. They all went to the right bowl. Could they see colour? Or was their own smell in their own bowl? It was an interesting experiment, but it didn't prove much.

A horse may shy because he glimpses things out of the corners of his eyes. Flickering images like shadows, and the sun through trees confuse him. The Indians used to pull out the eyelashes of a shying horse to give him clearer vision. We tried that with Showtime, who used to go perfectly for about half an hour, and then devastate you by shying so violently that he almost fell over. We cut his eyelashes very carefully with nail scissors. It didn't hurt him, but it didn't stop him shying.

There are two main theories about what to do with a horse who shies, and peers at things aghast, as if they were a personal threat to his safety.

One theory says, let him inspect anything he is afraid of. Make him go near enough to see it close and smell it. The other thinks that if you force him to go near something he doesn't like, he may be more nervous of it next time. So push him on. Ride him strongly. Give him something else to think about.

Your choice between the two theories must depend, as in all other horse problems, on whether he shies because he is really afraid, or because it is a habit, or because he is trying something on.

Barney hates to go out without any of the other horses. When you take him out alone, he peers and shies at so many things, both visible and invisible, that if you stop to let him smell them all, it takes a long time to get anywhere.

Things like drains or lines painted on the road that he will walk over unconcerned with the others, become unbearable terrors – My God, what is it, a *drain*? Brakes squeal as he steps a wide detour out into the road.

After having his vision checked, we decided that since he never looks sideways in company, shying is a device to avoid being taken out alone. So we push him on. Or don't ride him alone. My blacksmith, whose methods are rough, but successful, said we should take out a wide leather strap and belt him with it with a loud noise each time he shied, so he would be more scared of that than of the drain.

Did it work? I don't know. No one fancied riding down the village street, beating a bay pony with a leather strap and shouting, 'Har! Har!'

A ride is to enjoy. For the horse as well as you. Schooling work in a ring or a small field will give you better rides on a responsive and collected horse. But don't let him get bored or stale. Take him out. Give him variety. When you are out on a ride, work with him to make him do things right, but don't let it be work all the time. Slack off and let him look about him. Let him stand on a hill and stare into the distance like an Indian mustang.

Give him a loose rein and let him walk out with his head free. Sometimes a horse who persistently jogs can be brought down to a walk by just dropping the reins on his neck. This may speed him into a trot, but usually it works better with a jogger than continually nagging at his mouth.

If you keep pulling him back when he jogs, he gets behind the other horses and has to jog again to catch up. The whole business is exhausting, especially if he has a rough jog, so if he starts the jogging habit, try and get him out of it before it's too late to cure. Take him out alone and teach him the word 'Wa-a-alk', slowly and calmly. With others who walk fast, ask them to let you ride ahead, so you can set your own pace, walking slow, if necessary, but walking.

Then gradually get him to walk faster, by niggling with your legs at every step.

A horse who walks out free and fast, instead of poking along yards behind, or jogging to catch up, makes all the difference to the pleasure of a ride. A horse who walks well, gallops well, they say.

I went with a man to try a point-to-point horse in the rain. He walked him round the field with his collar turned up and his moustache streaming like a gutter spout.

'I'll take him,' he said.

'It's too wet to gallop,' the owner said, 'but aren't you even going to canter him, see how he moves?'

'I know how he'll gallop, from his walk.'

This story should end with the horse winning every race that season. It actually ends with his first day out hunting to qualify him for point-to-points. The man was right. The horse could gallop. He galloped through a hedge, hit a rail on the far side and was lame for the rest of the season.

He galloped all right. It was just that he didn't jump.

An alert horse who walks out well is less likely to stumble than one who potters and shuffles and pays no attention to what is going on.

When your horse stumbles unexpectedly, the shock to your nervous system can make you react with an angry jerk on the head he has dropped to regain his balance. If he stumbles a lot, cursing him and hauling up his head won't help. He doesn't stumble for fun. It may be no fun for you either, but it's worse for him, with your weight on top.

Examine his feet and legs. He may need shoeing. He may be slightly lame. He might even be anaemic, which can cause stumbling, but you'd need a blood test to find that out. If he is just sloppy and careless, it's your fault as much as his for not keeping him collected and on the job.

On an awkward rough place, or a bog, or a steep bank or thick undergrowth, most horses pick their way better without interference from the rider. If it's a squeeze through a narrow gate, or between trees, hang your leg along his shoulder in front of the saddle, so your knees and feet are not wider than his hips. He is not going to knock his own hips, but if he can bust your ankle or knee on a gatepost, or brush you off like a fly against a tree, he will have achieved what sometimes seems to be his life's ambition.

Unless he is a dreamer like Ben, he knows the way home and through the tricky places. He also knows where the galloping stretches are. It's a good idea, even if this is the only place you have really to gallop, to hold back to a collected canter sometimes, otherwise he'll charge off with you every time, unstoppable.

I hate to go riding with people who dash off full tilt every chance they get, wildly out of control. But galloping where you know the ground is open and safe, racing with other horses – ah, there is nothing like it this side of Paradise, or even the other side, unless we do get wings.

The horses enjoy it as much as we do. They get drunk on speed. To gallop fast intoxicates them to gallop faster.

Their wild ancestors ran together in herds, streaming over the earth's manless prairies. Running from enemies, and perhaps into unknown danger, the safe place was in the middle. That's why although your horse will strain to pass the others, if he gets too far ahead, he'll slow down and even turn his head. Where is everybody?

I am sorry for horses who are never allowed to gallop flat out. If we get such a thrill from just sitting on top of all that strength and speed, what must it be like for the horse to feel the power of his own muscles, the life and energy pulsing in the pounding rhythm of his stride that hammers the ground and flings it behind, rushing into the wind?

To gallop on purpose is a great joy. To be run away with is not, or to see someone else being run away with.

What can you do? If you are on a faster horse, you might be able to pass the runaway, turn it, or grab a rein, but chasing it will only make it run faster. If the ground is right, you may be able to cut through somewhere and head it off. Otherwise there is not much you can do but pray, and hope that the rider keeps cool and tries everything, except the fatal mistake of jumping off.

If you're being run away with, stay put. You are fairly safe to assume that the horse won't run himself into trouble. Fairly. But if you hurl yourself off at that speed, you are almost certain to be hurt.

Try and turn the horse in a circle, pulling hard on one rein. Turn him into a bank or a hedge, up a slope if there is one. Sawing his mouth doesn't work, but you can try slackening the reins, then suddenly jerking them upwards. Keep calm. Don't shriek and panic. Talk to the horse quietly. If he is used to your voice, some of it may get through his excitement.

When Jenny ran away with me, bareback in a halter, charging past her own field and on down the long, steep path that ended on the Cuxham road, I was small and panicky and I lost my head. I screamed and wept. I yelled her name. I yelled at God. I fell forward, clinging weakly to her mane and pleading to her with wrenching sobs, until she finally hit the road at the same time as a motorcycle, and they both swerved and fell down in a sideways slither.

# Chapter 8

Bow ran away with a friend of mine on the Royston Downs. It was a good place to do it, if it had to be done, on those long stretches of turf where they train the racehorses.

Bow, pronounced as in bow legs, had the official name of Bow Window. He was a thoroughbred hurdler, who had been bought by a girl in the next village to ride in the Newmarket Town Plate, the only race open to women.

I lived in Hinxworth then, in Hertfordshire, with ponies, because children came to me for the kind of weekends and holidays that had engrossed my own childhood in Oxfordshire.

When they ask me at the Last Reckoning to try to name one – just one tiny thing in my life that might have been worthwhile, I shall offer the claim: 'I taught a lot of children the love of horses.'

'No—' clutching the hem of the robe as its wearer turns away to mark the ledger. 'Not exactly taught, because it was born in them. But I gave them the chance to use it.'

So I had at various times Puck, Lollipop, Jacky, Peter, Titch, June, and others who came and went in the field by the Norman church, with the poplars along the stream by the bottom hedge. We didn't have proper stables then, only makeshift converted goat sheds. I wasn't looking for a horse, but they come to you when you are not looking.

Bobby came to me in America, just when I had decided not to keep horses for a while. His owner walked down the drive with him.

'He's wild. You can have him.'

So we built a stable and fenced some land and got another horse, and another, and the whole thing started all over again. Bobby was not wild, only temporarily unstrung by wild treatment.

Bow came to me in the butcher's shop in Ashwell, a beautiful place of white paint and sparkling tiles and baskets of blood-red geraniums.

There was a girl in riding boots, buying kidneys.

'I hear you're looking for a horse,' she said.

'Well, I—'

'I've got one for you to look at.'

'I don't really—'

'Won't take a minute. He's just across the road.'

He was beautiful, with gentle manners and a soft childish eye in a sculpted head.

'But I don't—'

'Just try him, at least.'

She knew I'd be lost if I did. Bow was like nothing I had ever ridden. He floated. He flexed to the snaffle in his soft mouth. He could canter at walking speed. You hardly needed to rise to his long level trot.

He was the first thoroughbred I had ever owned. I understood why some people will never have anything else. After I had him a month, I understood why the girl in the butcher's shop had decided to sell him and find something else to ride in the Newmarket Town Plate. Bow could gallop like Pegasus, barely touching the ground, but once in a while, not every time, and never when you expected it, he would switch off at a right angle without checking speed, while you sailed straight on without him. That was why he had been taken out of hurdling. He had done it in his last race and gone right through the outside rails, leaving his jockey on the course.

My friend is a large heavy man, not fat but weighty. He rides well, and Bow can carry him, and he loves to ride Bow.

I love to ride the black pony Jacky, but I don't often get the chance, since he always has a child riding him, or schooling him over jumps, or teaching him to stand with his front feet on a tub, or away on the other side of the hill visiting friends at Newnham or Radwell. But the children are at school now, except the youngest boy, who has been ill.

We start out with Bow and Jacky and Titch on an unexpectedly bright March day. My cottage sits under a lid of thatch so thick that you can keep dry in a rainstorm under the overhanging edge. My friend's wife, who is going to have a baby, waves enviously from the doorway and calls to the small boy, 'Don't overdo it.' The daffodils are bright gold outside the front hedge and clumped by the gate. In those days, nobody picked your flowers. I don't know whether they would now.

Beyond the loose box that I have made for Bow by filling in the

open cart shed, we turn off the lane on to a long grass track that winds through the arable land to Ashwell. The fields here are bounded by deep wide dykes, one of which we have to jump, because the wooden bridge is rotten and treacherous.

Bow won't always jump in front, but he'll follow the ponies anywhere. Jacky hates this dyke, and so do I. When I'm alone, I usually get off and lead the horse over.

'You can go first,' we tell the boy on Titch. No need. Titch is headed for the big ditch like a bullet, and the momentum of his speed carries him clear over from the top of one bank to the other. The boy turns in a circle to stop him, and looks back. 'Come on!'

I go at the jump bravely. Jacky braces himself to take off, and I hang on for the enormous leap with which he will clear the suspicious depths. Even with his hocks under him and his muscles tense, he changes his mind, stops, slithers half-way down the bank, cat-hops to the other bank and scrambles to the top.

Bow takes it more boldly, standing back and jumping wide, with his rider left sitting too far back, like old sporting prints of hunting parsons.

We canter fast over a field left fallow this winter, hop through a gap in the hedge and on to the road that takes us into Ashwell. Titch is still pulling, his Welsh nostrils squared like a dragon. He is too fat this winter, and not fit enough. Just as well.

'Don't overdo it,' the boy tells him.

Past two trim bungalows and the builder's sheds, round the blind corner by a high farmyard wall. As you clatter down the street, you can see yourself in shop windows, the butcher, the chemist, the draper, the plate glass window of the garage, checking your style like a dancer watching the practice room mirror. I see that my hair is like straw and I am too big for Jacky, but I don't feel it. His New Forest shoulder is good, and he carries himself well now that he is maturing. When we got him, at three, he was quite lethargic. He carried his head so low that you could have put a wheel on his nose to run along the ground.

Half-way through the village, we turn up by the dressmaker's house with cards of buttons and faded ribbon in the front window, and follow the cindery path that runs behind the back gardens and dustbins, crosses the road below the railway station and becomes – nearly fifty miles from where I rode on it in Oxfordshire – another stretch of the Icknield Way.

It is the same lonely, inviting ribbon of turf, winding now not between cow meadows and the wooded Chiltern hills, but through the open corn and bean fields that flatten out towards Cambridge-shire.

We do a fast canter side by side for about a mile, Bow not pulling at all, Jacky and Titch pulling, and curve up along the edge of the wide white pit where they dig out and process blackboard chalk. The boy gives it the evil eye and spits into the pit. As we ride round the top, the wind is blowing our way. The chalk dust rises in a powdery cloud, and settles on hair and clothes. Jacky's jet coat is silvered. Bow's long eyelashes are dusted white, and his rider is a preview of himself as an old man, with hoary eyebrows and mou-stache.

A narrow drop between blackthorn hedges, and the track widens again. The chalk dust blows away as we canter in the wind that blows across the flat open fields. The Icknield Way goes on, I don't know how much further, because we always turn off here, through two gates, past a deserted farm, and under the railway to get to the Royston road.

The brick tunnel under the line is damp and dark. The first time we discovered this way to get to the downs without having to go up the road and over the level crossing, none of the ponies would go through. We tried to ride them. We tried to lead them. Lollipop, Jacky, even Puck who had seen it all and normally was unsurprised, dug in their toes and snorted into the shadowy opening.

At last, with someone leading her and someone throwing earth at her from behind, Puck went cautiously through, with her knees bent and her stomach close to the ground like a scolded dog. She found a turnip on the other side and ate it noisily, holding it in her teeth and banging it on the frosty ground to break it. This brought Lollipop charging through the tunnel, and, after a struggle, Jacky. I leaned forward just in time as he suddenly dived through in a plunging scuttle.

He scuttles now, ears back. I lie on his neck until the change from the hollow sound of his feet on the stony path tells me it is safe to sit up. Bow is too tall to get through with a rider. On the other side, he won't stand still, and the man can't get on again.

'Train coming!'

He leads Bow to the embankment and climbs on from there, and we hurry away from the train. A real train, with half a dozen carriages and a driver shut into a far more sophisticated engine than Arthur Brewster's black and gold puffer that Jenny and I used to race at thirty miles an hour.

Across the main road and into the long grass, and the downs are rising ahead of us, fold upon fold away to the east, with the long turf gallops following the flank of the hills all the way to the golf course.

We decide to gallop to the first hill road and then go up to the edge of the beech woods to eat our lunch.

'Give me a start!' Titch has already started. Jacky goes after him. He stretches out his head and lengthens his stride. He and Titch are going flat out, as Bow comes up from behind in long easy bounds. For a moment we are all level, eyes streaming, hair, tails, manes, streaming behind us with the cries that spring unbidden from the throat when joy is too strong for silence. Then the splendid racehorse strides take him fast away.

'Pull up before the road!'

'I can't – can't stop him!' The man's voice comes back with the flying turf.

Bow gallops across the first road, on round the hill to the next long stretch, and across the second road. The track divides here. One side turns up the hill above the golf course. The other drops down to run straight and flat in the meadow beside the road. He swerves down there, still going strongly, and suddenly, with a bus load of passengers rubbing patches in the steamed windows to watch him, he makes his right-angled switch at full gallop.

From the higher ground behind, I see his rider fly sideways through the air like a parachute jumper. Bow is off up the hill, slipping on the clay, and the bus passengers crane back to see his rider sitting in the bomb crater he has made in the soft ground.

Bow gets half-way up the hill, then switches again towards the golf course. A man trying to play out of a bunker waves a club at him. He swerves back up hill, and at the top, he stops and turns to stare back at his conquered grassland, with his reins over his head.

The boy has pulled Titch up far back. When he reaches me, he holds the ponies while I go cautiously up to try and catch Bow. I think he will break away and gallop again. He is hardly blowing. But he stands and waits, and lets me get on Jacky and lead him quietly down the hill to his rider limping up.

'Are you all right?'

'Does he often do that?'

'I told you he might.'

'He never does it with me.' The young boy offers the age-old boast with which horse people annoy other horse people.

'When he does, I want to be there.' The man gets stiffly back on, and we eat our lunch as we ride towards home. We go back under the beech woods at the top of the hills, then down the long narrow lane which runs straight to the bottom of the downs. It is like the steep flinty road of Britwell hill, which used to take me back to that village on Jenny. There is a secure continuity to all these good rides, these agreeable countrysides, these willing horses who accompany the progress of my life.

We all have to go to London in the morning.

'Let's keep Jacky and Titch in tonight as well as Bow, and ride very early tomorrow.'

No ride is ever the last one. No horse is ever the last one you will have. Somehow there will always be other horses, other places to ride them.

# Chapter 9

When you ride with other people, you have to have what is called 'riding manners'. This means being aware of the others and their horses, making sure you all want to do the same thing at the same time, watching to see if anyone is having difficulty.

Don't selfishly hog the place at the head of a single file. Most horses worth their salt go best in front, so take turns.

'Prince Charming likes to go in front,' says his rider smugly, setting off at a brisk trot before anyone else can gather up their reins. 'Prince likes to go fast' is her excuse for haring off, out of control. Who is riding who?

Walk fast and canter slowly when you are leading. Look back at the others from time to time. If you are behind, keep your place. Don't push past the other horses and charge off ahead over the horizon, regardless of the chaos of fussed, excited horses you leave behind.

Don't gallop unless everyone wants to. The ride should be tempered to the most nervous, or least experienced, not the boldest.

But if you are the nervous one, don't ruin the ride for everyone else by screaming and raising alarms, or wanting to pull up as soon as they start to trot. If you're really that hopeless, you should stay in the ring until you can ride well enough to go out in company. No one should ride out until they can walk, trot and canter properly in a ring or field. When the 'ridden all my life' people want to ride your horse, try them out at home before you let them loose. You may find they can't even rise to the trot.

If you are the boldest one on the ride, don't lead the others over hair-raising jumps which are the only way out of a field, so that they have to follow, or go miles round and lose face. Don't show off. They will be too busy being scared to be impressed.

If you're in front, don't stop dead without raising a warning hand. If you're behind, try to keep a horse's length between you and the horse ahead. You've heard that before. It's one of the well-worn maxims which is easier said than followed. Like 'Don't catch a horse with oats', it is usually said by people who haven't got your particular problem. Even a kick in the chest doesn't seem to discourage the horse who always runs up on people's tails. And a bite in the rump doesn't seem to cure the one who kicks him. And it's often the rider's shin that catches the kick.

Out hunting, a kicker wears a red ribbon on his tail. In the show ring, he doesn't, so if you're in a big class, keep back from every horse, and let the air turn blue with someone else's curses, not yours. If you get behind infuriating competitors who canter so slowly that

your horse breaks to a trot, pass them, or cut across the ring to a space.

Riding manners include things like waiting for everyone to mount, and opening gates, and holding gates for the others to go through, and waiting for whoever shuts the gate. Staying off gardens and crops. Waiting at a road and all going across together. If one or two cross over ahead, it may be harder for the others to make their horses wait quietly for the next gap in the traffic.

If someone falls off, be sympathetic, but not hysterical. If it's you who falls off, sit up or get up if you're not hurt. Don't lie flat, giving everybody fits, and bringing your mother charging under the rail of the show ring – 'My child!'

They say that you have to fall off twenty-four times before you can ride. Or twelve, they say, if they have only had twelve falls. Some people manage to topple happily right and left, and land on their feet from all that practice. But for most of us, falling off is quite a shock to the system, even if you're not hurt. One moment you're on top of a horse, the next you're on the ground. Hard or soft, the geographical change is too sudden.

Don't say, 'He threw me.' Only a rodeo bronc deliberately throws the rider. Your horse may do something unsettling like stopping dead at a jump, switching direction like Bow, shying massively, bucking, or even rearing, but he doesn't do it to get rid of you. If you can't sit on, that's your affair.

If there is a choice between hanging on and letting yourself fall, hang on, unless the horse has reared so high that he may fall, in which case, slide off and get clear. If you are at that moment of truth, half in and half out of the saddle and clutching somewhere behind his ears, cling on and wriggle back somehow if you can. You're safer up there than on the ground.

Pessimists like the Sack, who always expect the worst, give up hope and let themselves fall. They even actually make themselves fall out of sheer defeatism. 'He threw me.'

When you fall, is it better to let go of the reins or hold on, to stop your horse going off without you? Hold on, I say, having walked home too many times without Jenny, or Little David, or Robert II, who jumped so big that you flew off like a drop of water on a hot griddle.

We entered him in some point-to-points one year. A man from Kenya called George rode him, but they never finished any race. George's wife and I would stand on a hill where we could see most of the course. When we saw Robert appear without a rider (once even without a saddle, when the girth broke), I'd say, 'Let's go and find George,' and his wife would say, 'The ambulance hasn't moved. Let's go and find the horse.'

Some people say that you shouldn't hang on to the reins when you fall, because you need to roll quickly away from the hoofs, and not risk getting dragged along the ground.

But your hands could let go. If you get dragged by a foot caught in the stirrup, you can't let go. It's the most terrible thing that can happen to anybody. Unless you are leading a riderless saddled pony some distance, never, never put the safety catches of your stirrup bars even half-way up. Leave them open all the time. Take both feet out of the stirrups before you dismount. You may be in the safety of your own field or yard, but if a sudden noise or movement makes your horse jump, you want to be either on or off him, not half-way.

The last word on riding manners is this:
Enjoy.
Enjoy the ride, and say so. If for some reason things go wrong, or you have been given a lousy horse, or you are riding badly, or your own horse is having an off day, which the best horse is entitled to occasionally, keep quiet about it. Don't gripe and grumble and try to spoil it for everyone else. Don't sulk fifty yards behind, so that they have to turn and shout at you, 'Everything all right?'

And don't answer, 'Horrible,' like the Sack. 'I can't do a thing with this horse.'

Too true. But it's not the horse who can't have a thing done with it. It's she who can't do a thing. No one wants to ride with the Sack, because she has no riding manners. She does everything wrong, and when all else fails to dampen the spirits of the other riders, she falls off and lies groaning in a bush, clutching her thick ankle and crying, 'Don't touch it!' before anyone has come near, while somebody sets off to catch her horse.

It's better to ride alone than with the wrong people. It's good to go out alone sometimes anyway, a very secret, individual and rewarding joy. You can sing, you can shout or make speeches, you can chat to the horse. You can go where you like, as fast or as slow as you like. You can go round jumps or over them. You need not wait for the stragglers. You need not follow the bold ones, pretending to be as brave as they are.

You are alone with your horse. You depend only on each other. Without the distraction of other horses and riders, he is more responsive to you, and you to him. You can teach each other many things. Communication grows. Understanding deepens.

# Chapter 10

I am going alone, with John in the trailer, to ride on Sandy Neck, a seven mile sandbar between the ocean and the great marsh on the other side of Cape Cod from where I live.

It is a day at the end of summer, with a deep blue September sky. The maples and locust trees are just beginning to hint at the golds and oranges and flaring autumn reds that will send people driving all over New England, taking photographs and crying, 'Will you look at that *colour*!'

You can only ride on Sandy Neck before the summer tourists have come, or after they have gone home to put their children back into school. The parking place is deserted except for the few cars of people surf fishing or walking on the dunes and the long curving beach, and one or two mad characters swimming in the icy waters of Cape Cod Bay.

John backs neatly out of the trailer, and after a small amount of difficulty with the saddle and bridle, because the ocean wind excites him, we start off with the dog Charlie along the wide marsh at the back of the dunes.

John flexes his black neck and steps out at once, two of his chronic coughs, then a series of healthy snorts to clear out his pipes. John is a quarter horse, just over fifteen hands, short-backed and springy, handily supple, with the pigeon toes of his breed and a rather thick neck disguised by his full glossy mane.

Jenny's neck was, as they say, set on upside down. Jacky was a bit ewe-necked too, before he learned to flex. John's neck is set on right side up, and so crested that when I bought him, with a stiff, untrimmed, hogged mane, he looked like a Greek horse on the frieze of the Parthenon.

Jenny, Jacky, John. Odd that they are all Js, my three best horses out of all those I've had. Not necessarily in breeding, but in character, personality, the amount of extraordinary pleasure we have had together.

The sand track round the marsh is soft in places, in others hard enough to trot and canter. Gulls and marsh birds rise from the wet land as we come round corners, following the curves of the dunes. In a patch of salty grass and stunted trees, all blowing away from the sea, a small fox gets up, and Charlie goes after it, yelping, but not catching it, although it runs quite slowly, and even stops on a rise and turns to look for him.

Once in Hertfordshire, I saw my dog Jo playing like this with a fox. They ran and jumped and circled all over a big stubble field. I thought it was another smaller dog, until I rode closer and saw that

it was a red vixen. One of the farmers told me that she and Jo had had – cuppies? pubs? He said he had seen them; but he was a man who saw many things, and had beheld a warning sign in the sunset the night thieves peeled all the lead off the old church roof, rolled it up and took it away in a lorry.

Half a dozen tiny cabins sit with their backs to the sand dunes, their rickety porches looking out over the wide green marsh. With no road, no water or electricity, no heat except the fires of driftwood they collect, some people live here until well into winter before they return unwillingly to civilization.

In a grey weathered shack all hung about with the coloured floats and glass balls and lobster pots that the sea has brought him, a man sits by a window. He has a beard and a thick pullover and a pipe, and a typewriter on the table.

We wave as I trot past, and I think we envy each other. He would like to be me out here in the sun and wind, instead of chained to a typewriter indoors. I would like to be writing there in such peace and stillness. What a place to write a book!

And yet, if one had all that beauty beyond the window, the birds and the changing colours of the marsh and its imperceptibly changing shapes as the tide seeps in and out, one might be too busy watching to write a line. If you want to write, it's better to shut yourself into a tiny room with a blank wall in front of you. Perhaps the beard and the pipe and the typewriter are disguises to make the man feel like a writer. Perhaps he isn't writing at all.

A sand hill hides his cottage from the sight of John stopping dead, and pitching me forward on his neck. Thanks for keeping your head up. Where streams under the dunes surface and run into the marsh, there are plank bridges, just two boards with a hole full of water between. A horse can't walk over them. John fusses and tramples a bit, finally jumps the bridge and stream quite neatly, and jumps the next one and the next and the next with less and less fuss. If we were going the other way, towards home, he would not fuss at any of them.

At the end of the broad spit of sand where the marsh opens out into the sea at Barnstable, we turn across the dunes towards the beach. The path runs through a struggling grove of flat-topped firs like a Japanese print, growing out of nothing but sand. One of the underground streams runs near the surface here. Charlie stops to dig, tail in the air, leaning on his elbows to lick at the fresh water which seeps through the dark sand where his paws have scrabbled.

Through a cut in the last steeper rise of barrier dune, with the sand blowing off the top of it into our faces, and suddenly it is a clean wind blowing as we come through the gap – and behold the sea!

It's low tide. Mile after mile, the hard wet sand stretches away on either side of us into the shimmer of distance, and before us over the rippled beach shining with pools to where the low breakers fall.

We turn towards the lighthouse at the far end of the beach, a fast canter splattering the wet sand, jumping rivulets, swerving round shallow pools. Then we turn and let go – you can gallop for ever on this beach.

Going so fast, lowering his back, streamlining his ears, his salty

mane blowing into my face, John doesn't jump the streams and swerve round the pools. He gallops right through them, splat, spatter, splat, and on to the hard sand again, both of us soaking wet, flying along the path of the sea wind.

... My horse a thing of wings, myself a god.

I let John gallop until he stops. There is no one on this beach but us. Far away, distorted by distance so that they seem to be hovering above the sand, a mirage of other horsemen is going towards or away from us.

We turn down to the sea, where Charlie has already splashed out, barking at a seagull. I take off John's saddle, and take the rein off one side of the bit, to have a longer rein to hold him with. He paws at the surf with his neck arched, blowing the froth off it like beer and splashing his stomach. Then he sags and goes down. He flounders on one side, gets up and goes down on the other side, his

thick tail lashing the water. Then he plunges out and goes down in the sand about half a dozen times. He can't get enough of this. He pulls back into the sea once more, then down on the beach to cover himself with the delicious gritty sand.

We walk up to where there is some coarse dune grass to eat, and idle in the sun till he is dry enough to brush the sand off his back and put on the saddle. Normally, he stands like a rock for me to get on, but now he turns as soon as my leg is over the saddle and we are off again across the drum-hard sand to the edge of the tide.

He slows to splash through an inlet to a long sandbar. At the far end of it, a dark mound like a rock becomes, as we canter closer, the body of a huge porpoise. John steps wide round it, snorting. Charlie, who likes to roll on dead things, can't find a place to start on this humped hulk, so he lifts his leg on it to show that he was there.

The sandbar runs diagonally back into the beach, and we cut up through the softer sand under the dunes, so as not to get mixed up with fishing lines. Beyond the ramp to the car park, a line of small cottages with steep roofs like Dutch houses sits along the dunes. I ride on a bit further, so as to be able to jump the breakwater, jump it back again – John going very fast, with his head down like a bull – and turn up between the cottages to ride back through the dunes to the trailer.

The sun is lowering. A woman in a flowered hair net and mauve slacks faces the slanting warmth in a long chair on the deck of her little shingled house, which has hearts carved in the window shutters, and is labelled Crow's Nest. As I climb the sandy path at the side, I hope she will open her eyes, because it will be nice for her to see something so picturesque as John and me, fresh from our long gallop in the sea wind. If I was basking on the deck of Crow's Nest, I would love to see a nice-looking horse come by.

She does open her eyes. She lets go a cry of outrage and jumps to her feet. The mauve slacks are short and tight, with little bulges at the knees like cricket balls.

'Get off my land!'

I pull John up. 'I thought—'

'That's the trouble with you people. You think you own it all.'

'I thought it was a path to the beach.'

'It's *my* path, and this is *my* house, and this is *my* bit of beach down to high tide mark.'

'Can I go through now that I've come this far?'

'No.'

'I'm not doing any harm. Surely a horse—'

'I hate 'em.'

My horse a thing of wings, myself a god!

Unwillingly, as I turn back to the beach to find another way through, I recognize the astonishing truth that there are people who actually don't *like* to see a horse go by.

Once when I was riding David at the edge of the sea, a woman told me that he was the cause of the polluted ocean, and no wonder the oysters were dying.

A man built a house and garage right across one of our rides through the woods to the cranberry bogs. There was no other way to get through, but you could just squeeze between the side of the garage and the thick pine trees. Or you could have, if he had not come hurtling out of his house, banging the screen door and scaring the horses, his face twisted with rage.

'Get off my property!'

'But this is the only way through.'

'I don't care.'

'Please?'

'No.' The conversation followed much the same lines as with the lady in the mauve slacks at Crow's Nest.

This was a summer colony of houses, so when the winter came, I thought he would have gone away, and we risked riding this way again. He hurtled out. This time he carried a shotgun, with language to match.

'I thought—' I tried to smile – 'I've always found all Americans so charming and friendly and glad to see people.'

'Well, lady,' he jerked the gun threateningly, 'at last you've found one who ain't.'

A family in a housing estate in Hertfordshire got two ponies, and fenced off and cleared a piece of waste land, and thought how nice it would be for the neighbours to have the ponies to look at instead of tin cans and old car tyres.

One of the neighbours used to sneak out at night, open the gate, and shoo the ponies out. Then she would scuttle back into her house again, and telephone the police to say that those dangerous, dirty, destructive animals were at large again, and must be got rid of.

The police didn't know what to do. On one side they had this violent woman, full of hate. On the other, a family of children who wept in the police station. It was very embarrassing.

I took the ponies for a while, and the violent woman became quite bored, with nothing to hate out of her back window, and no war to fight. She ran off with a travelling salesman, and the family took the ponies back.

In the car park, I unsaddle John and put on his halter. Usually I can lead him straight into the trailer, but sometimes he will back straight out again, unless there is another person to snap the chain behind him.

This is one of those days. There is no reason. It is just, like Showtime leaving his feed to dash out of the stable, to prove it can be done. Three times John walks in. Three times he backs out again before I can get the chain up. You can't tie a horse in a trailer before he is shut in behind, because if he pulls back, and then gets frenzied, as horses do when they start pulling back, he'll break his halter at least, if not his neck. When I'm alone, I hang a bucket of oats up front to keep John busy while I slip back to fasten the chain. Today I have forgotten the oats, and the hay net doesn't interest him.

There is a red sports car parked, but no one about. At last, as John is clattering stupidly backwards for the fifth time (Don't you *want* to go home?), another car pulls up alongside.

I ask the driver for help. 'Could you possibly stand behind him and fasten the chain while I—'

It is the woman in the hair net and mauve slacks. She has followed us to make sure we leave.

'—while I lead him in?'

She rolls up the window and turns on her radio.

The sun has gone down now behind the hills. The wind that blows across the marshes from the sea has a cold edge to it. The fishermen have gone. So have the people walking dogs. Except one. Far below on the beach, a small girl throws a stick for a big leaping dog. As I watch, a man's head comes over the edge of the dune. He climbs up and goes towards the red car.

When I ask him if he can help me, he is willing, but nervous.

'I don't know anything about horses.'

'If you could just fasten the chain behind him.'

'He'll kick me.'

'No, he won't.'

'I'm scared of both ends, but the back end is worse than the front.'

'You lead him in then.'

'He wouldn't come with me.'

'He would.'

'In *there?*' He peers into the trailer. He is a very nervous man, worry lines crumpling over a twitching eyebrow. 'He'll tread on me.'

'No, he won't.'

'He'll run me down.'

'You stand behind him then.'

'He'll kick me.'

We are back to where we started, when the child and the dog come panting over the top of the dune.

'She'll help you.' The man's face uncrumples with relief.

Chewing her long salty hair, the little girl, who is about seven, takes John's halter rope, clucks to him, and with the confidence of an old groom, leads him into the trailer. I snap the chain, and he doesn't even lean backwards to see if it is there, but at once begins to bully the hay net like a boxer's punch bag.

The woman from Crow's Nest has of course driven away before

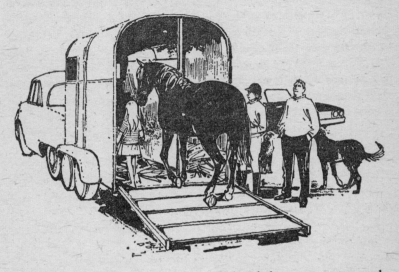

she can witness our triumph. The father helps me to put up the tailgate. The child leans out of the small trailer door to ask which way I'm going. 'I'll stay in here with him till where we turn off.'

It is illegal for people to ride in horse trailers, but she has shut the door, so I drive off, the red car following, with the big dog sitting like a person in the front seat.

At the crossroads, the child hops out and squeezes into the red car beside the dog. He is bigger than she is. She doesn't wave or smile as they drive away. Her face is still absorbed with John.

By the time I get home, it is going to rain, and the air smells of thunder. I shall keep the horses in tonight. I wash John down with warm water and scrape the sweat and sand off him. I clean the stables and fork in more bedding, put feed in the mangers and hay in the racks, fill the water buckets and bring in David, Ben and Barney.

After I've cleaned John's tack, I sweep down the tack room and the yard outside the boxes, not because it needs sweeping, but because I find it hard to leave the stable. I go into each horse again to stand with him while he pulls at hay, chewing juicily, pausing if I put my hand in my pocket to hear if sugar rustles in the lining, because he can't listen through the racket his jaws make inside his head.

I hang over John's door for a while, remembering our good day together. He has the loose box next to the tack room and feed shed, the first to be greeted in the morning, and the last to be left at the end of the day. What do they *do* out here at night? Eat and sleep. What do they think about? Nothing. They lead this mysterious, blank, contented life between the four familiar walls, staring into the night, moving their ears to far-off sounds, knowing that someone will come in the morning.

# Chapter 11

... knowing that someone will come. What if nobody ever came?

If a dog or a cat is abandoned, it can forage for itself somehow, or attach itself to another household. Even if it's shut up, it can usually make enough noise to be heard.

A horse doesn't neigh for help – except in films, where a recording of neighs is put into the sound track as needed. A horse abandoned is quite helpless, if his enclosure is too strong to break out. In a stable, he would die from lack of food, and especially water. Even in pasture, he could not survive if there was no water.

A man who works for the RSPCA told me how some horses had been found in a shed on a lonely farm at the end of an untravelled road. Their owner had got drunk in town one night, was hit by a car and taken to hospital unconscious with a fractured skull. For weeks they did not know who he was. No one missed him, for he had no friends or family. The local people never saw him anyway, so they did not know he was not at home.

Until one evening when a man and his son were out looking for a lost dog.

'Better not go on Duncan's land,' the father warned, but the boy thought his dog might have strayed to this lonely place, because there was always rotting garbage in the yard.

When they came near, they heard a banging, and they saw that the front door of the farmhouse had blown open and was banging back and forth in the wind. They went to shut it, and saw that the hall was full of blown leaves and branches, as if the door had been open for a long time.

'Didn't he have some horses?'

They looked in the shed. Three horses were imprisoned there in narrow stalls. They looked like skeletons. One was dead. The other two were dying. They had chewed all the woodwork within reach of their tied heads. There was nothing else to eat.

Thousands of years ago, when horses ran free in the wild, they might be killed by beasts of prey or abandoned by the herd when they were old and sick, but they did not suffer from man. We have taken horses from a life in which they could fend for themselves and made them completely dependent on us. We confine them behind a fence or a bolted door. We feed and water them. We are their source of life.

And so we have a tremendous obligation to them. A horse must come first. If you don't believe that, if you are not prepared to feed and take care of him before you do anything for yourself, then you shouldn't have a horse.

You probably wouldn't want one anyway. The people who want horses, the horse maniacs, enjoy the stable work as much as the actual riding.

Here you are coming home from a long ride at a swinging, loose-reined walk. The talk is of the ride, and how good it was.

Do the horses talk? They do when they are turned out together, breathing down each other's noses, or over a fence or a stable partition. But with bridles on, and under the control of a rider, they don't seem to communicate so much. When they are walking side by side, if you turn their heads together, they will often put back their ears in a biting face, even if they are good friends.

Back in the yard, you wonder if your knees will stand the shock of jumping to the ground. But it's not only your knees that make you not want to get off the horse. It feels so good up there.

You get down, and fend off the horse, who tries to rub his sweaty head on you, itching in all the places under the bridle. Don't let him. Your obligation to your horse doesn't extend to being a rubbing post. Apart from what it does to your clothes, sooner or later he is going to give you a tremendous zonk on the skull or the chin, and his head is harder than yours.

I used to ride with a girl who was passionately in love with Guy. She always let him rub his elegant head on her, as a token of her gratitude for the ride. We came back one day from a long hot ride, she got off, Guy made a lunge at her with his sweaty head, and she passed out cold at his feet in the stable yard.

It's good to walk the last part of a ride to bring your horse in dry, but don't panic if he is in a lathered sweat. Sweating is as good for a horse as it is for us, or for the dog to pant, which is his form of sweating. Working with a trainer in a ring, the horse was soaked in

sweat (and so was I), and I asked if I should walk him a bit before
we went on.

The trainer said, 'Don't be zilly.' He was a very German trainer.
'He hasn't begun to vork until he is zoaking vet. Now ve begin.'

When your horse is hot and wet after a ride, you can walk him
boringly around for an hour if you've got the time, or if, like the
Sack, you want an excuse to avoid the other stable jobs.

But it's better to put him out for a roll, as long as you don't leave
him out if it's too cold or wet. You can wash him down and scrape
him if it's warm enough. You can rub him down with a fistful of
hay or a rough cloth. If it's cold, and he's almost dry, you can put a
rug on him and let him steam gently into that. Straw or hay under
the rug will make air circulate and dry the sweat.

If you start rugging a horse every night in the winter, to keep him
from growing too shaggy (or because you like the look of him in a
blue and yellow rug with your initials in the corner), you've got to
stick to it. You can't put on a rug some nights and not on others.
Either let him grow his full coat, or keep the rug on till spring.

Give your horse a little water now, and don't forget to give him a
full bucket later, and more if he wants it. Feed him if he's cooled off
enough. Otherwise give him some hay to pull at until he can have

his oats and water. You can be mucking out or cleaning tack meanwhile. Wash off the bit, and go over the leather with a sponge and saddle soap and wipe off any loosened dirt. It doesn't take more than a few minutes, and it's much better to do a quick job each time than to leave it until you can do a major operation, which may be too late if you have really neglected the leather. Tack is expensive. Leather is beautiful. It's a crime to let it get filthy and dried out.

Put everything away in its place. Saddle on a rack. A short piece of board nailed narrow side up to the wall will do. Bridle on a horse-

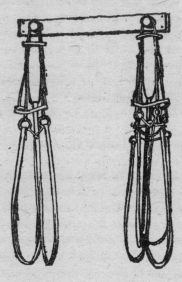

shoe hanger or a wooden peg (sawn off piece of broomstick), not a nail which can scratch the leather. Brushes, curry combs, sponges, gloves, whips – don't leave anything in the stable, especially if it is chewable. Don't leave things lying about where a dog can take them away to demolish. Let the dogs work on the hoof parings the blacksmith cuts. There is something in the substance that a dog craves. A piece of hoof is a puppy's best toy.

Everything is done. What a great satisfaction to have your horse fed and comfortable and all the stable jobs finished before you go indoors and try to get someone to listen to how good your ride was (almost as difficult as getting them to listen to your dreams, or the plot of a film).

You will come out later, probably, whether your horse is in the stable or the field. Night time visits are very rewarding. The horses seem extra gentle, extra loving.

Do horses love people? I think so, but in their own way, not ours. They feel comfortable and secure with their own people riding them and taking care of them, but it is mixed up with the fact that this person provides the food that keeps them alive. Horses, like all other animals, including humans, spend a lot of time trying to get enough food to put into their stomachs.

If as a tiny child you had a nurse or an *au pair* girl to look after you, you probably loved them, during that dependent time, more than your mother. A horse who is cared for by a groom will be fonder of the groom than of its rider. Taking care of your own horse brings you very close.

Does he think of you when you are not there? No one knows whether the brain of a horse, or even a dog is capable of reasoned thought about something that isn't there. The dog who pines for an absent master may be missing him physically more than mentally. He may not be consciously thinking, 'I wish he was here.' But the nerves of his body may be needing the feel of that accustomed hand. The hearing nerves are tuned to the pitch of that voice. The nose seeks the familiar scents.

The famous mourning dogs, like Greyfriars Bobby, who have refused to move from the grave of the dead master, may have been aware of some very faint trace of him, even through several feet of earth. A dog can detect an underground stream quite far down. Police dogs find buried bodies and well-hidden drugs.

A horse's sense of hearing is very acute, so he may hear you in the house, even if it is quite far from the stable. I used to think that John had ESP, because whatever time I got up, he would greet me from the stable even before I had run a tap or let the dog out. But possibly he could hear the sound of bare feet on the carpet, and it set his saliva juices working.

If John thinks of me when I'm not there, perhaps it is when his cavernous stomach rumbles. I need food. I want her to bring it. That 'her' connected with food may be the nearest he gets to an abstract thought about me.

Do horses remember people? A horse's memory is very good, when it is triggered off by a reminder: a landmark, a turn in the road, a familiar pressure of leg or rein, the sight, smell, sound and feel of a long-absent person. They do remember people, for ever perhaps, but again, in their own way, not ours.

In stories, the horse comes galloping miles over the prairie at the scent on the wind of the long-lost master. In life, some horses won't even lift their heads from the grazing, but an old friend's head and ears will go up at the sound of your voice. If you have been away, he will come at once to the field gate or the stable door and drop his nose into your hand.

'He knows me!'

He does, of course. He also knows that you probably have something for him in your pocket.

# Chapter 12

If you do it right, it works.

This is one of the basic truths about horses and riding. It doesn't mean that there is only one way to do everything with every horse. What works with one may not work with another, so if one thing doesn't work, try something else.

Take bridles and bits, for instance. Go into a big tack shop. Look through a catalogue. The mind boggles at all the different kinds of ironmongery devised by man since he first thought of putting something into a horse's mouth to control him better.

Snaffles, pelhams, bridoons, kimberwickes, sliding cheeks, egg butts, rubber mouth, twisted mouth, straight mullen mouth, port

mouth – they come in all shapes and sizes and degrees of severity. Finding the right one will make all the difference in the world to your horse.

If you buy a pony and the bridle comes with it, don't assume it's the right one. It probably isn't. The sort of bridle that people 'throw in' for the price of the pony is usually made of thin cracked leather, with no noseband and some totally unsuitable bit they happen not to want. A thin rusty snaffle on a hard-mouthed Shetland, for instance, with rings so small that when little Amanda pulls one rein, the whole bit slides through the pony's mouth and out the other side. What a disaster. The pony is miserable with discomfort, and slews off in the wrong direction with his mouth open. Amanda is miserable because she can't control him.

If your horse is not happy with his bit, you obviously can't go out and buy every other kind until you find the one that suits him. But save every bit that ever comes your way, and eventually you'll have a mixed collection in your tack room to experiment with.

Since the days when I only had the driving bit for Jenny, which was all wrong for her, and so no wonder she pulled my arms out, I have collected a great variety of bits which I take with me and add to whenever I move house.

Meanwhile, until you have got your collection of old iron decorating the walls of your tack room (or your bedroom if you are like that), borrow what you want to try, until you know what you want to buy.

Some horsey friend or neighbour will probably be willing to lend you a bit. Accompanied by a lot of free advice, because horsey people are even worse than doggy people for knowing what you should do.

'You don't want to put a curb on that animal.'

'Get him into a drop noseband, that'll do it.'

'Put a snaffle in that one's mouth, and it's Goodbye *you*.'

Try the new bit in the field or the riding ring first. Don't go straight out for three hours with a crowd of reckless gallopers, or it *may* be Goodbye you. Give your horse a chance to get used to the different feel of the bit and to find out how to react to it. If he has never had a curb in his mouth, you can't expect him to flex lightly and happily the first time he wears it.

The chestnut thoroughbred Rosie had been shoved on to the race track as a two-year-old without being properly mouthed. She used to make terrible yawing and chewing faces with a snaffle, chucking it about like a deck tennis quoit. When someone tried her in a light pelham, she started to back as soon as she felt pressure on the curb rein. She continued to go backwards at a great rate all round a field until she crashed into a tree. After that, we took all bits out and rode her in a hackamore. You could stop her, but not turn her. After she had swerved uncontrollably out into the main road traffic, we sold her for breeding.

Whatever bit you are trying, keep your hands as light as if they held a raw egg. Imagine the reins are fine thread that will snap if you pull too hard. Never forget that the horse has metal in his mouth. Imagine what that must feel like. If your imagination won't stretch that far, put a bit in your own mouth and pull on it hard, or get someone else to. I did that once to a heavy-handed boy to show him what he was doing to the horse. He never came back to ride any more.

Start with the gentlest possible bit. Try a snaffle first. If your horse has a light, unspoilt mouth, preserve it like a jewel. If horses were sadistic enough to imagine punishments for people, they would invent a special torture for anyone who ruined a young horse's innocent mouth.

If your horse's mouth has already been made hard by severe curbs and heavy hands, you may be able to improve it with a lighter bit and lighter hands. It will take time, but it can be done.

A horse that pulls and is hard to hold doesn't necessarily need a stronger bit. Sometimes, the stronger the bit, the harder he pulls against it. If the bit is paining him, instead of flexing his neck and dropping his chin and slowing to avoid the pain, he'll fight it.

If you want to see what a horse looks like in pain from a severe bit, watch a Western film. As soon as the rider reins in his horse, up goes its head with the mouth open. The longer the cheek of a curb bit, the fiercer the leverage on the jaw. The long-cheeked Western bits are terribly severe. As soon as he feels pressure on the reins, the horse chucks up his head to try to avoid the jag.

When I found my quarter horse John, he had been broken to a Western bridle, and already at three years old, he was afraid of the bit. In the dealer's stable, he had smelled me all over my head and face and hands at great length, a good sign of a curious, clever horse who likes people, and I had the feeling we were meant for each other. I tried him out in a pelham, and although I loved the feel of him, and knew I wanted him, he fussed with his head all the time.

'Why does he fuss so with his head?'

The dealer was leaning on the gate of his field, observing me without enthusiasm. 'You're hanging on to him too tight.'

People who are trying to sell you a horse always say something like that.

'Why won't this horse go straight?' you ask.

'He will if you use your legs properly.'

'This horse is forging.'

'You haven't got him collected.'

'He's very hard to hold.'

'If you pull at him, he'll pull at you.'

If there's anything wrong, it's always you, not the horse.

When I got John home, I started to un-Westernize him. Besides teaching him to walk and trot, because he wanted either to jog or

103

canter, I had to find a bit he wouldn't fight. A snaffle bothered him at first. He chucked it wildly up into the corners of his mouth. A standing martingale brought his head down, and he began to respond. It took months to get back his confidence that he wouldn't be hurt. In any crisis, or difference between his ideas and mine, up went the head, with the eye rolling.

I love the way he will stop on a sixpence at speed. You don't have to touch his mouth. You just yell, 'Ho!' which is American for Whoa, and hang on for the dead stop. But his head goes up automatically, and I hate the thought of the wicked Western bit that taught him to do it.

He still is more at home with a straight bar in his mouth than a jointed snaffle, so he now wears a rubber-mouthed kimberwicke with a leather curb chain.

Just after I wrote that, I took John out, and we met a posse of small children on hairy ponies chasing two others with dangling reins and empty saddles, their riders stumbling behind, blinded by mud and tears.

John was deranged. He whipped round with his head going one way and his body another. He stuck his jaw down and leaned on the rubber bit, and was altogether vile. I took him out the next day in a snaffle and he was perfect.

You never know. There are no fixed rules. It's not only different things with different horses, but different things with the same horse.

John will go beautifully for weeks without a martingale, and then suddenly start to chuck up his head. Perhaps it's me. One doesn't always ride the same.

If your horse, like John in his head-chucking phases, throws up his head a lot, or carries it 'star gazing', so high that he can't see where he's going, use a standing martingale. Fit it so that you can raise the horse's chin about as high as his withers. It won't interfere with his jumping. His head stretches out, not up. It will help, by keeping his head in a place where he can look properly at the jump.

Some trainers go rabid at the mere mention of martingales. 'Get his head right by schooling, not straps!' they thunder. Well, all right, but meanwhile I'd rather use a martingale than get a zonk on the nose when the horse flings up his head. Especially if he's got a bristly hogged mane. That really hurts.

Incidentally, if you are teaching beginners to ride, put a martingale or at least a neck strap on the horse while they are learning to rise to the trot. They can hang on to that instead of the reins, and it will help to keep their balance forward. Beginners tend to get left behind, and they lose their balance and their hands fly up and they either fall off, or jerk the horse in the mouth, which is worse.

Get as good a saddle as you possibly can. Making do with a cheap lump of junk that doesn't fit either the horse or you is the stupidest way to save money. You can't sit properly in a rotten saddle. Don't make that an excuse for bad riding. Save up. Find a job. Sell something. Get a decent saddle.

A secondhand one of a good make is better than a new, inferior one. A forward seat saddle with a deep seat and good knee rolls is the most comfortable, the best help to a good seat, and essential for jumping.

Take good care of all your tack, and it will last you a lifetime.

Your saddle, like a favourite chair, will get better and better for you as time goes by.

I knew a woman who had a saddle for thirty years. She grew into it and it moulded itself to her shape and way of riding. One day some idiot left it on a stable door. The horse knocked it on to a stone floor and broke the tree. The local saddler sniffed at it and drew down the corners of his toothless mouth, and said it was past repairing.

'I've thrown it away for you.' He was an arrogant old saddler, who did things his way, not yours.

The woman went out to his rubbish heap at the back, took the saddle home, and buried it behind the hay shed with loving ceremony, like the good friend it was.

So much for what the horse is going to wear. What about you?

You don't have to dress to the teeth every time you go riding, but you do have to look neat. You do have to look reasonably horsey, not all hung about with chiffon scarves and dangly earrings, like a woman who rides past my window with her toes down in fancy high-heeled boots with tassels. Sometimes she wears a hairpiece of false yellow curls, which does at least make her hold her head up, to keep the curls in place.

Riding in shorts or jeans and gym shoes looks casual and fun, but unless you ride bareback, it's agony. The stirrup leathers pinch your calf and the inside of your knee gets sore if you grip. In ten years' time, you'll have broken veins all over the inside of your legs, which won't look a bit attractive. You may have them anyway, after years of riding, but they won't be so bad if you have worn breeches or jodhpurs with strapping. Those are the only things to ride properly in, and jodhpur boots, or full length riding boots.

No one can use their legs properly without boots, because it hurts too much. You may fancy yourself as the spirit of free natural youth in your patched jeans and dirty bare toes, but you aren't sitting right, and you can't possibly be gripping.

If you ride a sluggish horse, spurs can be a help, as long as they are blunt ones without rowels, and you know how to use them. Not as a substitute for your legs, but as an extra. Not all the time, but on the occasions, like a show, when you really need to wake a horse up and keep him going.

You have got the right kind of saddle and bridle on the horse and you are wearing the right kind of clothes. Take a ride past a big shop window and check how you are sitting. Get someone to take a photograph, or better still, a film of you on your horse.

Are your toes just visible below your knee? Are your stirrup leathers the right length? Take your foot out of the stirrup and hang your leg down straight. The bottom of the iron should just knock your ankle bone. Stand in your stirrups. You should just clear the saddle. Your knees should be well into the knee rolls, with the inside of the thighs supported on either side of the pommel.

Two words describe a good seat. Relaxed and proud. Head up, shoulders down, heels down, elbows in – you know how to sit, but keep it supple. Not stiff. Not sloppy.

The sack of potatoes is slumped there on a horse resting a back foot, with rounded shoulders and her chest caved in, and half an acre of countryside visible between her knees and the saddle. Her boots are dirty and cracked because she never polishes them, her hair is hanging over her disgruntled face, and her whole attitude says, this is all a great bore and I think it's going to rain.

But there you are proudly in the place where you would rather be than anywhere else in the world, on the back of your good horse,

and your whole attitude says, look at us. Aren't we a terrific partnership?

Proud and relaxed. Also quiet. Watch really good riders. They have complete control over the horse. They can make him do anything, yet you hardly see them move a muscle.

A lot of shouting and waving arms and legs and whips about never gets anybody anywhere. If you are riding well, it should look easy. It isn't, of course, but only you know that. If you've got an impulsive, restless nature, try to calm it. It may make you exciting company with people, but it will make you upsetting company for your horse. Quiet-natured people ride better than violent ones, even if they are less technically expert. The horse goes quietly for them. They leave him alone.

A friend who hadn't ridden for years came out with me on lively, free-striding Ben, who will bounce about and plunge his front end up and down if you ride him too tight and tensely. After the first trot and slow canter, she was quite at home with him, and he with her.

'I'm out of shape and out of practice,' she said, 'but I thought if I didn't bother him, he wouldn't bother me.'

Sometimes if a horse is fussing, jogging all the time, snatching at the bit, dancing sideways, and in general making an ass of himself, when all else fails, you can try just dropping the reins. Don't bother him and he won't bother you. That sounds like a dealer trying to sell a badly-behaved horse, but it does often work.

Guy used to jog all the way home, straight up and down in a very rough jog that was good for the figure and the liver, but exhausting. I tried everything with him. Pulling him back on his hocks, turning him in circles, walking him back the other way and trying to turn ahead still in a walk. Nothing worked.

'Try dropping the reins,' someone suggested.

I did. Before I could gather them up again, he had dashed me through a thin hedge and down into a gravel pit as steep as the side of a house.

But that was Guy. He did everything the hard way, and actually hated a loose rein. If he pulled and you pulled him back, he leaned contentedly on the bit and went faster.

You know if you are riding well, because the horse will go well, and you feel right. There will be days when it all feels wonderful, and you think, at last, I believe I really know how to ride. Then the next day, for some reason, you can't do a thing right. That's part of the fascination. It is never quite the same, and you never know it all. There is always more to learn, more to enjoy, until the end of your riding days.

When you think you know it all, save up for some really first-class riding lessons, and find out how little you do know. Never stop learning. Never stop discovering. Never stop trying to improve yourself, and your horse. What a terrific partnership . . .

# Chapter 13

The more you work with your horse, the better the partnership will be. Continual basic schooling at home will enormously increase the enjoyment of all your riding, for both you and the horse.

If he is already well schooled, you should go on with his training to keep him right and to learn with him how to be better. If he is rather young and inexperienced, a 'green' horse, you have a wonderful opportunity to develop him to the right habits and way of going. If he already has some bad habits, from lack of training, or bad handling, they can be overcome by careful retraining. It may be long and slow, but it's worth it. There is no horse in the world that can't be improved by patient, understanding schooling.

Don't expect success at once. You are not going to transform him, or yourself, in a few days.

Suppose, for instance, he won't lead with the inside leg when he's cantering in a circle. Don't give it up after two days as hopeless, and stop doing circles, or allow him to go on lolloping clumsily round leading with his outside leg. Make your circles smaller. Vast sweeping expanses are no good for schooling anyway. Keep things fairly small and concentrated in an enclosed field or riding ring where the horse will pay attention, and can't get going too fast. Canter in only one half of the ring. Start by jogging him in a tiny circle, and use your outside leg strongly to squeeze him into a canter while he's still on the tight turn, so that he has to lead with his inside leg, or fall down.

Vary your methods. If one thing doesn't work, try another. If he is still on the wrong lead, don't keep hauling the poor thing in and starting off again with the same signals. If he knew what you wanted, he'd do it. If he is confused, constant stopping will make him more confused and frustrated. Finally, he may not canter at all on either lead.

Keep him interested. Horses get bored like people. Don't just slog round and round with the same old walk, trot and canter. There are many basic things to practise. None of them are difficult, though all are difficult to do well, like anything that is worth working at.

Figures-of-eight at a trot, then at a canter, trotting a few steps in the middle until he gets his change of leads smooth enough to start to learn a flying change. Turns on the forehand, with your legs doing almost as much work as his, and his front feet turning as closely as possible on the same spot. Trotting over poles laid on the ground. Backing through a right angle, or between two posts. Opening and shutting gates. Following a simple basic dressage course – walk to one marker, sitting trot to the next, slow canter in small circle, extended trot between diagonal corners – to make the horse change his speed and his paces at definite points, not just any old time he gets round to it. A good riding textbook will explain to you in detail a dozen simple things you can work at.

Don't always school the horse in the same field or ring. Find some nearby space to practise in different surroundings. We sometimes go to a small plot of grass up the road which belongs to a man who used to be a trainer. He lets us use the plot because he likes to see the horses, and because it gives him a chance to come out and tell us what's what.

He has all sorts of old wives' tales concerning phases of the moon, and diseases like strangles and grass staggers and poll evil, and a diet of wholemeal bread and cigars to keep the inside of your horse as healthy as the outside.

If we have a new horse, it has to go up the road for his approval. I don't tell him I've actually bought it, until he has run his hand down its legs, looked in its mouth, snapped his finger by its eye, poked it in the ribs and given it his OK.

'She may do, in time. Needs a lot of work to get her into shape. Bring her up here tomorrow, and we'll see what can be done.'

When he is not masterminding my horses, he runs outdoor auctions of furniture in a corner of the grass plot. Sometimes both activities at the same time.

'What am I bid for this four-burner gas stove, perfect condition – *get that horse on his toes!* – only one owner, glass oven door, look here, you can see in, the food can see out – *on his toes before you ask him to canter!* ...

'Here's a set of nice little period chairs, five of a kind, what am I bid? – *trot him out, he's pottering* – don't ask me where the sixth chair is, lady, if I had six you couldn't buy 'em for the miserable money you folks – *heels down, girl, you look like a monkey* – you folks are bidding for this quality merchandise ... eighteen, eighteen, do I hear twenty? *That horse is going to sleep!*'

Lungeing your horse is a good way to get variety into the basic schooling, and give him exercise in a short time and a small space.

If you haven't got a proper lungeing cavesson with a swivel ring on the noseband, you can get a large ring with a split in it, which can be opened with pliers and closed again round the noseband of a leather headstall or a strong halter. Fasten the snap or buckle end of the long lungeing rein on to the ring, and it will move from side to side as the horse changes direction, so that you don't have to keep going up to him to move the rein over to the other side.

If you need to handle the horse, always stop him on the outer circle, and you go to him. Don't call him in to you, or he may get the habit of turning in to the centre whenever he feels like it, or thinks he might have earned a snack.

If he doesn't know anything about lungeing, get someone to walk on his outside and lead him round, while you turn on the same spot in the middle keeping the lungeing rein taut. He learns surprisingly quickly to stay out on his circle, and will quite enjoy this simple sport, moving freely, yet under control. Don't use a whip unless you are expert. Pick up a little bit of earth and throw it behind him to get him going. After a few throws, you will only have to reach your hand down slightly and he will move into his trot or canter. Tell him, 'Ter-*rot*!' very clearly, and '*Can*-ter!' using a recognizably different rhythm and note of voice.

Don't carry on round and round in the same direction for ages. You will both get dizzy, or the horse will get sick of it, and stop or pull away.

John lunges beautifully, with his relaxed rocking-horse canter, front feet rather wide apart, broad-chested and slightly pigeon-toed like all good quarter horses. His heart isn't in it though. He will canter on command for exactly twelve rounds each way. Then he does his famous dead stop, turns and looks at me.

'Do I have to go on with this childish business?'

The skewbald pony Oliver had to be lunged in the winter when his child was away, because he was too small for me to ride. He would whizz round at full gallop, bucking and squealing, and when he had had enough, would pull the rein through my hand, taking some of the skin, and head for the gate. After the second time, I learned to wear gloves. And shut the gate.

Always shut the gate before you start to lunge. Remove temptation. Think ahead. Avoid trouble where you can. That applies to everything you do with horses.

Don't wrap the rein round your hand. You can sprain, or even break fingers if the horse pulls out. Watch where you put your feet. If you get your legs tangled up in the long rein, anything may happen.

Lungeing is good for voice training, and voice training is very important, whatever my friend at the auction sales thinks.

'Five fifty, I'm bid. Five fifty for this brass fender – *Legs, girl, use your legs, not your tongue!*'

You can easily teach your horse what 'trot' and 'canter' mean, by saying the commands when you are riding, as you give him the signals with your legs. But use your voice together with hands and legs, not as a substitute. If you only say, 'Trot' or 'Canter', he may obey, but it will be pretty sloppy. Horses who go to a lot of shows learn to change their paces when the ring steward or the announcer gives the commands; but if the rider just sits there like a passenger, it won't be very impressive.

Don't go cluck-cluck with your tongue and teeth. This is strictly taboo, don't ask me why, unless you are driving a horse in harness, or lungeing, or moving him over in the stable. A little chirrup with your lips to coax him into a canter is allowable. Cluck-cluck to make him trot is absolutely out.

Voice training is handy for gymkhana events. A pony that will slide to a stop when you say, 'Whoa!' can win you the musical chairs. But in jumping classes, shouts of, 'Hup!' are horrible. Usually superfluous too. The Hup merchants, even quite well-known riders, sometimes give voice to it when the horse is already off the ground and half-way over the jump. Perhaps it is an involuntary reaction, like a belch or a hiccup.

Even worse than a hupping rider is a hupping spectator, some goon in a porkpie hat standing by the biggest jump and yapping, 'Hup!' at the wrong moment. Who is riding the horse? It's enough to give it a nervous breakdown, getting advice from all sides, as well as on top.

When you are getting down to the really hard, intensive schooling, it is better to do it alone, especially at first, when you may get into a few battles. Don't get into a battle unless you know you can win. Don't tackle more than you can cope with. It's better to drop it than to fight on, with the horse getting more stubborn or more flustered, and you getting more and more angry.

Anger and animals don't go together. Anger doesn't go with anything, for that matter. Even though it seems to be caused by something or someone else, it is actually caused by you. You want something – a horse to obey you, a jar lid to unscrew, a friend to like you best. You don't get it. You get angry. It's not the horse or the jar lid or the friend who caused the anger. It's you.

If you find yourself losing your temper with a horse, get off. If things are not going well, chuck it for today and try again tomorrow. If things are going well, stop while you're ahead. Don't try 'just once more' to prove something or other to yourself.

If you have had a good training session, and your horse has behaved well, and it's time to stop, pay no attention if someone comes out just as you are going in and says, 'Show me what you've been doing.'

If you do, it probably won't go right again. It seldom does, in my experience, when people come to watch.

I taught a nervous child to ride for a month, and she was doing quite well, until one day a car drew up and out poured Mother, Father, Cousin Nellie and little Lewis, come to see the show.

You can guess what happened. The child and pony had been jumping two foot six quite nicely. We played safe with eighteen inches. The child looked at her parents instead of the jump, the pony ran out, and the child fell off. She even managed to break her collar bone, which she never would have done if nobody had been looking.

Although, like my Olympic friend who shot the cackling spectator out of the tree with a water pistol, you need to do a lot of your basic schooling unobserved, it is also good to vary it by working with friends and trying different things together.

Line up the horses and do exercises in the saddle, standing in your stirrups, turning your body, touching your toes, lying back on the horse's rump (not on Ben's, it bucks).

Ride without stirrups. Knot your reins and ride without them. Drop the reins and stretch out your arms as the horse takes off over a small jump, and feel how much more fluidly your balance follows his. Bring out a radio and do musical rides. Play follow-my-leader. Jump in pairs, side by side and tandem. Change horses. All these things are good for control and obedience, and for increasing the confidence between you and your horse.

Keep the training varied. It's work, but don't forget to have fun.

The girl who owned the show hack Honour Bright would never ride him outside the ring. He was called a hack, but she would never hack him. When we once persuaded her to ride out with us, and see what she was missing, she moaned all the way, 'Oh – he's losing his manners!' (as if it was a shoe or a tooth).

She took a short cut home and never came out again. Which was a pity, because although Honour Bright performed with automatic perfection in the ring, he was only leading half a life, and so was his girl. He was a beautiful horse, and they could have had fantastic rides together if she had let him stretch his wings sometimes and be more free and easy.

Ring work should be varied with rides. Each one helps the other. When you go out for a ride, you can make that a continuation of your horse's training, at least for part of the ride.

Let him relax and enjoy himself. Let him stretch his muscles in a gallop once in a while. Even let him play up a bit, prancing about for fun and showing off. But when you collect him up and tell him to do something, make sure that he does it.

Don't let him lose the obedient habits you are teaching him in the ring by letting him do what he likes when he's out. If you tell him to trot, don't let him swing into a canter until you decide that's what you want. If you tell him to canter, don't let him break his stride into a trot. You can feel when he's going to break. The rhythm changes slightly and the shoulder muscles tense to throw out that first trotting foot. Use your legs at once, especially the one opposite to his leading leg, and keep him cantering.

You decide where you'll go fast and where you'll walk. Never canter on the road. Trot slowly, and try to keep on the softer verge, if there is one. Don't always canter or gallop in the same place. A good horse will always go faster when he meets the challenge of a steep hill, but don't let him always charge off in a bounding canter to get to the top. Make him walk up it sometimes. It's better for his muscles.

Don't let him eat. Once he gets the habit of snatching at leaves on trees and bushes, it's very hard to cure.

Bobby, with his strong arched neck and impulsive ways, was the worst eater I ever had. He not only plucked and chewed as he walked, with festoons of greenery dangling from his bit, but he would turn his head at a trot and clamp his jaws on a fresh spring branch, while his legs trotted on and he almost broke his neck.

Eating grass is even worse than snatching sideways at bushes. Don't let your horse drop his head to eat every time you are standing still. Soon he'll stop of his own accord, and suddenly there is nothing in front of you as the head disappears downwards, and you're lucky if you don't go with it.

Small ponies are the worst for this game. They get used to being ridden by children who aren't strong enough to keep their heads up. If you have this problem, tie a piece of strong twine to the top of the pony's bit each side. Pass it through the loop of the browband and fasten it to the D at the front of the saddle, just tight enough to give him freedom with his head without being able to get it down to the grass.

Let your horse understand a definite difference between on duty and off duty. Wandering about the field or the stable yard, he can be an off-duty slob and do what he wants. On duty, saddled and bridled, he is under orders. You have always got to be the boss.

That doesn't mean tyranny. It still means partnership, but if the rider is not in control, nothing works.

Fortunately, a horse doesn't mind being bossed, in fact he prefers it. This is why there is no limit to what we can achieve with him. His herd instinct is to obey a leader. You are the leader, as well as the food-bringer. If horses can love, which I believe they can, it is for both those reasons.

# Chapter 14

Is a horse a natural jumper? He can jump quite high by himself, though he hardly ever does, and if turned out in a field with jumps, he will chew them, or knock them over, but never jump them for fun.

By himself, an untrained horse jumps too fast, with a flat back, not using his muscles or picking up his feet, and probably hitting the jump. Unless it's a huge fence, which he wouldn't tackle alone anyway, his jump is not much more than an extension of his canter.

A horse has got to be taught to jump properly, with control and judgement, arching his back and using his muscles the right way. If you want to teach him to jump, you have got to help him to develop the control and the judgement and the muscles.

This is not done by whacking him over enormous jumps. You start low. Very low. An untrained horse is naturally afraid of a high or difficult jump. The way to overcome his fear is by constant slow practice over low jumps, going higher very gradually, building up his physical power and his mental confidence in himself and his rider, so that in the end he will jump anything you ask him. That's how the top show jumpers get there.

Jumping is exciting and fun and marvellously good for both you and the horse in the development of this terrific partnership, with which you are going to conquer the world.

But if you don't want to jump, don't jump. Don't do anything you don't want to, just because you are afraid of being thought a coward.

Be a coward if you are one. Don't spoil your enjoyment of riding by forcing yourself, or letting someone else force you to do anything that scares you. I'm a bit of a coward myself, and so naturally I pretend that cowards are the people with more imaginative and sensitive natures than the bold ones.

However, if we will start slow and low, we too, like our horses, can overcome our nervousness. If we do it right, it will work, and if it works, we shan't be scared. I wouldn't want to be never excited and scared though. You would lose half the adventure of life.

Confronted with a jump, an untrained, green horse will naturally speed up, because the faster he goes, the less energy he needs to get him over.

Any horse can jump fast. You are going to teach your horse to jump very slowly. If he has always been cantered over jumps until now, or allowed to rush at them like a bull, it's going to take some time to slow him down. But it can be done, with the old steady and patient routine. Once you have got him slowed down to where he will jump from a walk, then the real training begins.

Set up a low pole about eighteen inches from the ground. Each end should be supported on opposite sides of the uprights, so that you can jump it either way, and it will fall if the horse hits it hard. Don't have a pole so flimsy or so lightly fixed that it will topple at a tap of his hoofs. For safety, it should fall if he makes a bad mistake and stumbles over it; but if he just knocks it through carelessness, it should be firm enough to knock him back. Next time he'll pick up his feet.

Having set up your pole, don't go to the other end of the field and make a great lot of important preparations, so that the horse is a nervous wreck before he ever gets to the jump.

The Italian dictator Mussolini, who was a coward as well as a bully, and had to scare people before they could scare him, used to sit behind an enormous desk at the far end of a long room. When people were summoned into his presence, they had to walk an endless length of carpet under the glaring stare of this deranged tyrant, so that by the time they arrived before his desk, they were quaking with nerves.

Don't make a big Mussolini deal out of any jumping. Even when the jumps get higher, don't make an elaborate presentation, so that the horse thinks, Hey, what's up? Don't run at it from miles away. Make your approach quite short, especially when you are doing this very slow work. If the horse seems nervous, walk him round quietly, and perhaps lay the pole on the ground and let him step over it several times until he's at home with it, before you put it up.

Walk up to this low jump, perhaps trot the last two paces, and then hop over it, standing in your stirrups with your weight on your

knees and your hands well forward, both you and the horse completely relaxed. Stop and turn quite soon, and go back over the jump
in the same way. Don't make vast circles round the jump again. Pull
him up in a few paces, turn, and keep on going back and forth over
the jump until the horse (and you) thinks nothing of it.

At this point, he will probably get careless and hit the jump. This
is good. It's good for a dog with no road sense to get gently bumped
by a car and find out that cars hurt. It will be good for your horse to
rap himself a few times on a pole that is heavy enough to hurt.

When he is used to this first low jump, set up several other small ones at odd angles, and just potter about, hopping over them in different order and different directions, sometimes at an angle, using quite a loose rein once he has slowed down completely. Almost any horse, however excitable, will eventually calm down with this quiet, relaxed practice.

All the time you are jumping from a walk, you are exercising and strengthening the muscles of his back and quarters. When you raise the jump, the speed will have to increase a little to get him over it with the same amount of effort. But don't use more height and speed until you are both ready to learn to pace and time the approach and take off.

Keep him at this slow business for a while. It's a bit boring, but it's the only way to do it.

Even after you have progressed to a whole course of higher jumps and a faster speed, keep going back to the basic training. Don't be like the schoolgirl who was asked by a new teacher why she couldn't do multiplication sums.

'Oh,' said the girl, 'we did multiplication last term. We're on algebra now.'

While you are doing this low, slow work, try different things like knotting the reins and dropping them before the jump, riding with one stirrup and with no stirrups. You are developing your own muscles as well as the horse's. Leg muscles and balance are what makes the difference between a rider and a passenger.

Keep your hands well forward, or drop them down the sides of his neck. Whatever you do and whatever happens, don't jab the horse in the mouth. If you think he's going to jump big and you may get left behind, grab a piece of mane to keep your hands forward and down. If you do get left behind, drop the reins, fall off, anything. If you jab the horse in the mouth, he won't jump any more.

In the olden days before the discovery of the natural seat, and later the forward seat, riders used to go over jumps sitting far back with their legs stuck out. Look at any old print of sportsmen taking fences in the hunting field. Top-hatted and whiskered, they are all sitting back like Grand National jockeys landing into the drop at Becher's Brook. The horses have all got their ears back and their mouths open. I can't imagine how they got them to go on jumping. Perhaps by galloping over the fences flat out. There is a great deal of whip flourishing in the old sporting prints.

If you train your horse with patience and slow care, he will hardly ever refuse or run out. But sooner or later, as the jumps get more difficult, he is going to do one or the other, and probably both.

To generalize (which one should never do about horses, because they are all different), running out round the end of the jump is usually disobedience. Refusing by stopping in front of it is usually fright, though it can be laziness, or the rider's wrong approach.

To overcome his fear of a new, strange jump, your horse must develop confidence that you aren't going to put him at anything impossible. Properly trained, he should jump anything you ask him, familiar or strange. That is the ideal you're aiming for.

Some people, even quite advanced riders, make a great to do about 'showing' a horse a new fence before they try to jump it. This shouldn't be necessary, and it can even make things worse, if you ride him up to a jump and then turn away without jumping it.

At a small pony show last year, they let the competitors into the ring before the class, to show their ponies the jumps.

One girl rode straight up to each fence as if she were going over, stopped dead, tried to push her fat roan pony's head down to see it and smell it (which he couldn't care less about), then hauled at the reins and turned him away. When it was her turn to compete, the pony was expecting to be pulled up before the jump. He refused the first two, and had to be whacked over the third from a standstill before he settled down and jumped the end of the course as easily as he could have taken the first three, if his rider hadn't messed him about.

The last fences were brush jumps anyway, and before the event even started, much of the greenery had been eaten by the ponies of small children 'showing' them the course.

If your horse has the habit of running out at fences, you must be very, very firm. Remember who's boss. It's better not to jump at all than to let the horse decide whether to jump or not. Give him an inch and he'll take you into the next field. Don't let him get away with it.

If he runs out to the left of the jump, don't turn him further round to the left to come at the jump again. Make him turn the way he didn't want to go. If he runs out to the right, turn him back hard to the left.

Come back into the jump as quickly as you can. Don't, like the Sack, flop to the ground and kick pebbles, or ride the horse back to the rail to ask the spectators if he isn't a mean and rotten brute. Don't take him miles back from the jump and do the long Mussolini approach, so that he has time to swing out and avoid the jump again. Bring him in from two or three paces, and push him over, even if he knocks the whole thing down. If it's low enough, which it should be until he is cured of running out, he can jump it from a standstill anyway.

At the next jump, keep the reins tight until he has actually begun to take off, then give him his head when it's too late to run out. Keep him slow. If he does run out or refuse, you are much less likely to fall off.

If you're afraid of falling off, you probably will. If you're afraid that your horse is going to swerve out fast, or stop dead and pitch you over the jump on your own, he probably will do that. It's true what they tell us cowards: if you are nervous, the horse will sense it, and be nervous too.

But it's no more use telling people not to be nervous than it is to tell them not to fall in love. If you're in love, you're in love. If you're nervous, you're nervous. It's not your fault. You didn't ask for it. It happened to you.

You can't be bullied out of it, but you can gradually overcome it yourself by all this slow, pottery hopping about over tiny jumps. Just as the nervous horse eventually won't be scared any more, so you will find to your surprise and delight that you are, if not bold, at least not frightened any more. What were you afraid of? Jumping is casy (that's when you bite the dust in the real crusher, so don't get carried away).

As in all horse dealings, avoid trouble where you can. If the horse runs out, use wings. Poles resting between the jump and the ground will do. Take them away when he is more secure, because wingless fences are better, but if he starts to run out again, put them back. Why have a war when you can have diplomacy?

If you are really having trouble and you absolutely cannot get your horse over a jump, pack it in for the day; but before you do, make him jump *something* even if it's only a pole on the ground. If the jump was higher than usual, put it down low to get him over it. Never let him get away with anything.

If your horse or pony is good enough and you want to train him for a show, which you should when you are both ready, because it's fun and gives you something to work for, he has got to get used to jumping anything at home – worse things than he will meet at a show.

Make up some fairly low, but varied and quite fearsome jumps, and keep changing them. We spend a lot of time at the local dump, picking over the fascinating things that people chuck out. Oil drums, old tyres, bedsteads, sofas, doors, bicycle wheels, broken gates. You name it, we have them all.

We were coming out of the dump, pulling the open trailer with which we deliver manure to organic gardeners. It was full of old iron, broken ladders, a kitchen counter top covered with flowered linoleum, a useful-looking table without legs, which was going to be part of our wall.

The dump man, who is called the Disposal Superintendent, stopped us on the road driving out.

'You're going the wrong way to bring that junk to the dump,' he said.

'We're bringing it away.'

'It takes all kinds.'

And it takes all kinds of jumps to get your horse ready for anything he may meet at a show.

One of the girls had been taking the palomino David to a few of

the small local shows. He was young and inexperienced. He could jump fairly well, but he was timid in the show ring and had never yet got round a course.

We unloaded the manure trailer and got to work. With the flowered linoleum counter and the table top and oil drums and an old red stable rug, we made a terrifying jump, with bicycle wheels at both ends, a flag flying from one and tinfoil streamers from the other. It was fairly wide, but not high. David could jump it easily, if he would.

Somebody started to count the refusals. I think it was fifteen before they stopped counting. At last, as dusk was settling in, the girl grew desperate and determined at the same time. With her legs working like mad, she got him over.

Nothing to it. They jumped it half a dozen more times in the fading light, then did some rounds the next day, with the horror jump as part of a course. When they got to the show, the plain white poles of the novice course were child's play to both of them, and they came fourth. It would have been better, but the jumps were such child's play that David didn't always bother to pick up all his feet.

When you set up a course at home, whether it is plain bars and hurdles and brush fences, or junky monstrosities which do nothing for the looks of your field, but wonders for your horse, you can work at establishing a good rhythm round the jumps.

Work out different courses, taking the jumps in varied order and from both sides. Plan ahead how you are going to approach each one, straight and in the middle. Think where you are going before you get there. As you land from one jump, start looking at the next. Begin with a small circle to get into a slow, collected canter. Accelerate for the last three paces before each jump, and recover the smooth collected canter rhythm between jumps.

If you make a mistake and are coming into a jump wrong, or your horse is getting slightly out of control, take a circle round part of the field and come back smoothly to the jump. The horse won't know the difference, and you won't lose the rhythm.

There you go under the trees by the gate, trotting correctly with your hands down and your horse alert, swinging into your smooth canter without anyone seeing you move a muscle (if anyone was watching). Round your small circle, and his ears prick as you straighten him into the brush jump – gorse and hedge clippings stuck between two boards. You lengthen his strides, one, two, three, over, with your head turned to look at the hurdles even before you turn the horse towards them.

Over the hurdles, over the wall made of logs and two painted doors, over the fallen tree trunk – the easiest jump, but he comes carelessly in too close and has to hop it – nice wide turn round the oak tree to bring you straight on to the pole with the wheelbarrow standing under it. The second small brush jump, partly eaten away when the ponies were turned out, hurdles with a striped pole on top, the in-and-out made of oil drums and old tyres, the angled in-and-out where you jump a bench into a corner of the field, stop, turn and jump out over hay bales, and down to the triple bar, low but wide.

He stretches. You give him lots of head. He lands clear with a flick of his tail, and you canter back to the gate, where the rooks fly out of the tops of the tall trees, clamouring and scolding.

A perfect round. It was *good*. He can do anything, this horse, with you, and you with him. What a partnership!

# Chapter 15

Showtime, who boarded with me for two or three years, was a very fine jumper. The first time we took him to a show, he won a third in Open Jumping, and everyone was delighted with him, until he went on strike against the trailer.

He had loaded all right in the morning, but for some reason, he absolutely and completely refused to go home.

The show was over. Everyone else had gone, or was loading their horses into boxes and trailers and pulling out over the trampled field.

It was evening. Shows round here tend to go on for ever, because they never start on time, and the same horses are often entered in two classes which are going on at once. A class in one ring will be held up for an hour because two of the entries are waiting to jump in the other, especially if they belong to any of the people who are running the show. Then it's lunch time and everybody goes away and drinks beer.

It was getting dark. Any horse with a grain of sense and decency would know that it was time for a free ride home and a large meal. Not Showtime. The longer we tried, the more stubborn he became. It was not the stubbornness of panic, like Genie, who would lean back on the rope and freeze into a sort of paralysis from which she not only wouldn't move, but couldn't. Showtime was quite calm and relaxed. He simply would not be led, pushed, coaxed, driven, or kidded into the trailer.

Finally, when it was quite dark, four men who wanted to close up the show ground and go home put their arms round the square, stupid horse, and literally carried him into the trailer.

We were thankfully on the road when another driver slowed alongside and shouted that the trailer lights were out. The connection had broken going over a stone. We had to wait an hour until a car came from home to travel close behind the trailer and hope not to meet the police. It was almost midnight when we got home. Showtime had eaten all the hay in the net, and was dreaming happily, leaning against the partition. He did not particularly want to come out.

With every horse problem, you have to try to find out the reason, and then keep trying different things until you find one that works.

Showtime's problem turned out to be that he didn't like seeing a person ahead of him in the trailer. So we fastened a long lungeing rein to his headstall, passed the other end of it through the trailer and out of the front window, and he allowed himself to be pulled gently in by unseen hands.

If the horse seems to be really afraid of the box or trailer, the best thing is to park it in the field where he is turned out, and let him get used to it as an everyday affair, like a tree.

After Barney fell in love at the Falmouth show and went berserk in the trailer and cut his face on the front window and skinned his hips charging out through the side door, I thought we would never be able to get him into it again. Even if we could, I thought I would never have the nerve to drive him.

I was ready to give up, but Barney's child said No. We couldn't let ourselves be defeated by a fourteen hand pony. Besides, she wanted to take him to another show.

We put the trailer in the field, with the ramp down. We left Barney there by himself when the other horses came in for their evening feed. We put Barney's in a tub at the bottom of the ramp, and after walking round for a while, snorting and bulging his eyes, he put his head cautiously into the tub and ate.

Gradually, a little further at each feed, we moved the tub higher up the ramp. First he had to stand with both feet on it, then with all four feet and his head inside the trailer, then with two feet in the trailer, then with four, with the tub right up at the front. Then one of us held the tub so that his head would be in the right position to tie up. Then we fastened the chain behind him. Then – it had taken about two weeks – we tied him up and left him there for a while after he finished his feed. Then we led him in and tied him up without the feed.

It wasn't exactly greed that cured Barney. It was habit and routine. A horse adores routine. He likes everything done at the same time and in the same way and the same place. Barney got used to the trailer as the harmless place in his field where he stood quietly and had his regular feed at regular times. We don't have to lure him with oats now. The trailer has become a familiar part of his world, and he will follow his own familiar child inside.

The lure of oats up front only works with a horse that is willing to go into the trailer anyway, or a horse like John who will back out again if there is no one behind to fasten the chain. If he is being stubborn, even a greedy horse will pay no attention to the food.

There are a lot of other things to try to get him inside, and a lot of things that he will try to stay out. I know them all, alas.

If he will lead up to the trailer, but not move forward into it, someone standing behind with a whip, but not necessarily using it, will sometimes get him going. Or they can chuck a small handful of earth or grit at his quarters. That works better than a whip. It surprises him without scaring him. Once he is scared, you've had it. The whole business has got to be very calm and quiet, with as few people as possible involved and no shouting or rage. A horse who won't load is infuriating, but if you get angry, go and kick a bale of straw, not the horse. If you get violent, so will he.

You can fix a long rope to one side of the back of the trailer, and someone can walk round behind his quarters to try and push him in. Or two people can have two ropes and cross them behind him.

My extraordinary young blacksmith, whom all horses respect but not fear, puts a long rein through the headstall, passes its buckle end over the back and round under the tail and fastens it round itself at the side, so that the horse's bottom is in a sort of sliding loop. When he leads the front end of the horse forward, he is pulling on the end of the rein that is also pushing the back end. The horse may kick, but there is no one behind him.

You need to be very strong for this, but it does work. I've seen this young man, who has a magical, but down-to-earth understanding with all animals, pull a big, heavy, obstinate horse up a steep ramp into a truck. Then he brought him out, and led him in again. The second time, as soon as the horse felt the rein tighten round him, he walked up the ramp under his own steam.

If your horse persistently swings out sideways, park the trailer alongside a hedge or fence, so you've only got one side to worry about.

Even if he doesn't dodge out to the side, it may be difficult to get him to step on to the ramp. Give him time to look into the trailer, and adjust his vision to the darker interior. A horse's eyes react rather slowly to a change of light. That is one reason why he may be suspicious of going into a strange stable. It's darker than outside, and at first he can't see what's in there.

If he won't move forward, get someone to pick up a foot and put it on the ramp. When he relaxes and puts some weight on that, pick up the other foot and put that on too. If he steps back with both of them, try it all over again. Eventually, when he gets used to the sound and feel of his feet on the ramp, he will go in.

That is the one good thing about a horse who is obstinately difficult to load. Eventually, if your patience can hold out, he will give up and go in.

Ben had one of the most irritating tactics of evasion. He would pull his head sideways and refuse to look at where he was supposed to be going.

'Trailer? I don't see any trailer.'

You walked him in a circle, and as you brought him forward again, up would go his handsome head and he'd stare all over the landscape, with you dangling on the end of the rope.

Sometimes it worked to take the rope tight round his nose, or into his mouth and through the noseband, or over the top of his head to get more control. Often he still pulled his head away, and if you weren't wearing gloves, the inside of your fingers went with it. With Ben, you had to allow about half an hour extra for this 'I don't see any trailer' routine. Then, just as you were ready to give up the whole project and put him back in the stable, he would suddenly droop his head, sigh, and walk meekly up the ramp, his dark blue eyes melting with virtue.

I was very glad of those four strong men who picked up Showtime and carried him into the trailer in the dark, but often, if you can't load your horse at the end of a show, it can be more nuisance than help when other people get into the act.

And they do. It's like a street accident. If you are having any trouble, a small crowd collects at once and tells you what to do.

'Take the whip to him.'

'Let him wait, don't rush him.'

'Don't get in front of him.'

'Don't get behind him.'

'You'll never do it that way, girl. Where's your long rope?'

'Leave him alone and he'll go in by himself.'

'Give him to me, the beggar.' A large hand takes the rope from you. 'Come on, get up there, you devil, what's the matter with you!'

'Don't frighten the poor thing.' A woman with a gipsy scarf over birds'-nest eyebrows strokes the horse's nose and coos at him, 'Poor lamb, what did they do, eh?' to give the impression that she is the only one who cares about the unfortunate animal.

A man comes back from his horse box flourishing a long whip. Another has pebbles and curses to throw. Once with Guy, a beefy man who had elected himself Chief of Operations got so infuriated that he tore a rail out of the fence and beat him on the bottom with that.

Clonk. Guy shot inside, and the man had the ramp up behind him before he knew what had happened.

'Thank you.'

'Sorry to be so rough.'

'But it worked.'

'Sometimes if you do it all wrong,' he bent to pick up the fence rail, 'it works.'

# Chapter 16

You can't take a horse straight out of a field, brush off the mud, and take him to a show.

Even if you don't expect to win anything, and are only going to the show for fun and experience, you must prepare for it carefully and well at home.

Give your horse slow, steady exercise and increase his grain a bit to match the work. It's the two together that make him fit. More work, more feed.

Work with him hard in the ring, but don't keep slogging him every day in the same old circles and over the same old jumps, or he will go stale. Set up one or two jumps that are more difficult than he'll meet at the show, but continue to do the basic low, slow work.

Keep him in for a night or two before the show, and get him as clean and sharp-looking as you can.

With a horse that is turned out most of the time, and is always down squirming in mud or dust patches, washing is the only way to get him really clean. This will shock the elbow grease brigade, who think it should all be done by exhaustive grooming; but if, like me, you can't spend as much time as you'd like in the stable, you will take a few short cuts, and be glad of them.

If you use soap, be sure to rinse it all out. Get as much water off him as you can with a scraper, and brush him when he's dry. Wash his mane and tail. Borrow clippers if you have none, and trim his heels and his beard and his ears, if he'll let you, and the place behind his forelock where the crown-piece of the bridle goes. If you can't get clippers, do the best you can with sharp scissors.

Plait his mane the night before the show. If you have to struggle with it on the show morning, you may end up late, and in a temper. Wet hair is easier to plait. Needle and strong thread looks better than rubber bands. Decorations of coloured wool on a pony look awful.

If you haven't pulled his tail neat and narrow at the top, never try to cut it or clip it. When it grows, it will stick out sideways and look horrible. Plait it by bringing thin strands of hair from the sides,

which bind it with a braid down the middle. If you are no good at plaits, get a horsey friend to show you, or better still, to do it for you.

I knew a twelve-year-old girl who didn't ride and wasn't much interested in horses. But she was very interested in making money. After she had witnessed some of the agonies and frustrations going on at her family and friends' stables the day before a show, she learned how to plait manes and tails quickly and skilfully, and hired herself out at ten pence a mane and fifteen pence a tail (five pence danger money).

Clean all your tack. Collect everything together the night before, so you won't forget vital things in the morning. Make sure your clothes are clean and correct. It's rather expensive to be properly turned out, but if you want to go even to a small show, it's necessary.

It used not to matter, long ago in the days when I started showing, first hairy Chips, and then Jenny, who was an absolute whizz at gymkhanas, but leaped the rail of the ring the only time I jumped her, and nearly killed a child in a push chair.

I found an old picture of her and me getting a sixth place rosette at Princes Risborough. She is wearing the driving bit with buckled reins, no noseband, a hogged mane growing out, and a tail all fuzzy at the top where she rubbed it. I am wearing some strange baggy garment that looks like plus fours, a shrunken jersey, Wellingtons and no hat.

In those days, at the beginning of time and horse shows, it didn't matter. Now it does. If you don't look right, you'll feel wrong and you'll ride wrong. And they won't even let you into the ring without a hard riding hat. If you have been jumping without one at home anyway, you are not only reckless, but foolish.

When you get to the show, don't start cantering your horse or pony round and round in circles 'to get him calmed down'. Horse shows are very tiring. Apart from his classes, he is going to use up a lot of extra energy peering at new sights and being excited about the other horses.

Ride him round a bit to get him relaxed and supple if you've brought him in a trailer. Don't take him over and over the practice jump so that he gets bored, and no one else has a chance at it. If you have worked properly at home, a couple of practice hops and a little gentle schooling in a quiet corner is all you need.

Don't ride near cars. It's too dangerous. I saw a child leading her pony between two parked cars when someone inside opened a door right into the pony's shoulder. Robert's rider took him to the car to get her lunch. Something scared him and he backed, and caught a hoof in someone's front bumper. A man got it free by wrenching the bumper loose, but the fetlock was badly cut.

Don't jostle the spectators. They have as much right to be there as you. Don't barge through the crowd, stepping on sandwiches and toppling people off camp stools, or shouting at them to get out of your way, like a French aristocrat riding down the peasants. Don't ask someone in open-toed sandals to hold your restless horse for half an hour while you disappear to the ice-cream tent.

When your friends arrive and beg you to let them get on the horse, say No. If you are going to let anyone else swank around on your horse – which I wouldn't, but you may be kinder than me – don't let it be until after he has finished his events.

Watch the other classes and the other competitors, to learn from what they do, both good and bad. Watch the judge to see what pleases him. If, as it turns out later, it doesn't happen to be you who pleases him, don't blame the judge. He may be slightly prejudiced in small ways, but he is, after all, human, although disappointed competitors won't admit that. At the next show, you may meet a judge who is prejudiced in your favour. Then you'll be glad he's human.

If you are going to jump, learn the course and memorize it until you could jump it with your eyes shut. It's amazing how many quite good riders throw away their chance by going off course.

While you are waiting your turn in the collecting ring, watch everyone who goes before you. You can learn a lot. Move the horse quietly about to keep him alert. Don't let him stand resting a leg and half asleep until your number is called and you suddenly gather him up and ride him into the ring in a fog – 'Where am I?'

Let's face it. Even though you are only there for the experience, or the competition is so good that you know you haven't got a hope, there is always the secret dream. The miracle might happen. It would be pointless to go to shows if you didn't dream of winning, or at least being placed. The aspiration, the ambition, this is the excitement.

But if you get nothing, don't sulk. If they divide the sheep from the goats in a big showing class, to concentrate on the potential winners, don't collapse if you are eliminated along with the goats. The glum faces that ride out of the ring are distressing in a country that is supposed to be noted for its sportsmanship.

The cheery smile that hides the breaking heart. The 'Here goes nothing' grin. That's the spirit that will one day bring you prizes. That and more work.

If you don't win anything and you think it's not fair, don't tell the judge so afterwards. Asking what was wrong can be helpful to correct mistakes, but he is usually very busy, and most people who pretend to be asking what they did wrong are really lodging a complaint.

Don't bother the judge, unless he offers you advice, which the best ones will do at informal shows and, for heaven's sake, don't let your mother tackle him.

I saw a stout woman with a red face and legs like furniture stride up to a small woman judge and demand, 'What's wrong with my pony?'

'Which was your pony?' the judge asked politely.

'Number 104. The bay with white socks. Girl with pigtails.'

The judge consulted her card. 'Oh yes, nice pony,' she said, still polite, 'but I didn't like his way of going.'

'What do you mean?'

'It's hard to explain. It's just something about the way he carries himself – you know?'

'No,' said the woman. 'I don't know.'

'Look, really, I—'

She was trying to get back into the ring to judge the next class, but the stout woman was in her way, blocking the gate. 'I'm not complaining. I'm asking for advice.'

'That'll be the day,' said the judge, suddenly delightfully rude, ducked round her and under the rail into the ring.

Almost as bad as showing displeasure if you don't win is not showing pleasure if you do. You may never have this problem, but if you do start winning, don't ever lose the delight.

I watched a very competitive Best Rider class, where the six excellent finalists had to change horses, and jump a course, and do quite complicated individual performances.

The girl who won was marvellous. The next girl had ridden well, and should have been proud to get a second among such competition.

She rode out in a slouch, glowering under the peak of her cap.

'What did you get?' a friend called to her. 'I didn't see.'

'A lousy second.'

'Good for you.'

'Big deal.'

Thank goodness she didn't get a first.

Good luck to you in everything you do. Even if you never win anything at a show, have fun. Enjoy yourself. There is no point in it otherwise. And if you do win, remember that it wasn't all you.

It was you and your horse.

You and your horse. His strength and beauty. Your knowledge and patience and determination. And understanding. And love. That's what fuses the two of you into this marvellous partnership that makes you wonder, What can heaven offer any better than what you have here on earth?

And talking of horses ... there are three of them out in the field with their heads over the gate, and a rising wind heading towards a chilly night. It's time for me to go out and feed David and Barney and John.

## Christine Pullein-Thompson's Book of Pony Stories 50p

An anthology of pony stories from well-known writers. You will find all sorts of stories – sad, exciting, funny, even ghostly – about all sorts of horses.

## Christine Pullein-Thompson's Second Book of Pony Stories 45p

Another stable-full of stories – exciting, funny and even mysterious – enough to thrill anyone who loves horses and ponies.

James Aldridge
## The Marvellous Mongolian 40p

Tachi, a young stallion, is taken from the rugged mountains in Mongolia where he was born and sent to a nature reserve in Wales, but he escapes and starts the long trek back home. Peep, the gentle Shetland pony, goes with him. This remarkable story is told through the letters two boys write to each other – Baryut from Mongolia and Kitty from Wales.

Some pony stories by
Christine Pullein-Thompson
## Strange Riders at Black Pony Inn 35p

It looks as if the Pemberton family are going to have to sell their
house and horses as it is all too expensive, but instead they take
in paying guests. But soon after the guests arrive, the trouble starts –
somebody has a grudge against them.

## Mystery at Black Pony Inn  35p

The Pemberton family land in big trouble in this adventure at Black
Pony Inn. The smiling 'Commander' with his elegant Mercedes
seems perfectly charming, but is he really?

## A Pony to Love 35p

Do you want a pony of your own?
Or do you already have one?
Whichever it is, this book is a basic guide to everything you need
to know about buying, owning, feeding and caring for a pony,
and there are cartoons too, just to keep you smiling.

also by Monica Dickens:
## Summer at World's End  35p

The Fielding children are still on their own, still caring for any animal in distress. Lack of money is a problem, while some unwanted visitors add to the fun – and the excitement.

## World's End in Winter  35p

More adventures of the Fielding children, with their family of animals. Their first winter at World's End is packed with incident and excitement that involves children and animals alike.

## Spring Comes to World's End  35p

As their Uncle Rudolph threatens to deprive them of their beloved World's End, the Fielding children try to earn the money to buy it themselves. But money disappears as fast as it comes in, and it is not until the children are at the point of despair that their home is saved in a dramatic and exciting climax.

## More books by Monica Dickens:
## Follyfoot 40p

Here we meet for the first time the people and horses who live
at the farm on the top of the hill. There's always so much to do on
the farm – tending unwanted horses, providing mounts for film
companies, schooling ponies, helping unlucky holidaymakers and
keeping a wary eye on the unscrupulous owners of the Pinecrest
riding stables : life can never be dull for Callie and her family !

## Dora at Follyfoot 40p

More exciting adventures at the Follyfoot farm ! This time, the
Captain has to go away and he leaves everything in the charge of
Dora and Steve, warning them – with an eye on the finances –
'Don't buy any more horses !' But Dora knows she just has to buy
Amigo, the rangy, scarred cream-coloured horse, even if it means
borrowing money. And to pay the money back, someone from
Follyfoot will have to win the Moonlight Pony Steeplechase !

## The House at World's End 35p

Rather than stay with relations in a grey London suburb, the
Fielding children, Tom, Carrie, Em and Michael, decide to live by
themselves in a tumbledown country pub. There are thrilling
moments and frightening ones, too, as the house at World's End
becomes a haven for sick, stray or ill-treated animals.